History of Ethiopia

A Captivating Guide to Ethiopian History

Free Bonus from Captivating History (Available for a Limited time)

Hi History Lovers!

Now you have a chance to join our exclusive history list so you can get your first history ebook for free as well as discounts and a potential to get more history books for free! Simply visit the link below to join.

Captivatinghistory.com/ebook

Also, make sure to follow us on Facebook, Twitter and Youtube by searching for Captivating History.

Table of Contents

Introduction

Ethiopia has a long and exciting history. People have lived there for millions of years; in fact, it is one of the earliest homes of Homo sapiens. However, a fully-fledged kingdom didn't appear until around 980 BCE.

D'mt was the first true Ethiopian kingdom, but it paled in comparison to the Kingdom of Aksum, which emerged in the 1st century CE. This kingdom was home to trading routes, diverse people groups, and resources that other nations desired. It became so influential that many consider it one of the world's greatest powers at that time.

Typically, people know about the Roman Empire or the Persian Empire, but not as many know about the Kingdom of Aksum, which certainly rivaled these nations on the world's stage. This book aims to change that.

Of course, Ethiopia's history continued on after the Kingdom of Aksum fell. We will talk about the various rulers who oversaw the country and the changes they brought about while discussing the larger global situation and how it impacted Ethiopia.

This is an exciting ride—one you will not want to miss. Traverse the annals of history with us as we dive into Ethiopia's past.

A map of modern-day Ethiopia.

Chapter 1 – From Ethiopia's Origin to Its Golden Age

The moment that Ethiopia entered recorded history still sparks some arguments among scholars. But one figure that many have long pointed to as the first mentioned Ethiopian monarch is the legendary Queen of Sheba. This is still highly debated, with some even arguing that the Queen of Sheba wasn't Ethiopian but actually from Yemen or some other nearby region. Nevertheless, there are those who believe that the Queen of Sheba was an Ethiopian monarch, and her story presents us with one of the first recorded renderings of Ethiopian history.

Regardless of the deeper discussion at hand, let us dive into the account of the Queen of Sheba. Our source for the comings and goings of the Queen of Sheba is none other than the Holy Bible.

Some might scoff at the use of scripture for establishing the historical record, but biblical writers have been accurate in many other historical instances that have been fully corroborated by both archaeology and other sources from antiquity. At any rate, in the Bible's Book of Kings, we first find mention of the Queen of Sheba.

The Book of Kings tells us of how the Queen of Sheba heard mention of the great and powerful ruler of Israel, King Solomon. She was inspired to gather up her court and make the grand trek from the Ethiopian highlands, up through Egypt, and on to Israel to meet King Solomon himself. This event was also mentioned in passing in the later New Testament, more specifically in the Book of Matthew, which spoke of the "Queen of the South" coming to meet Solomon. The "South" is generally believed to be in reference to Ethiopia, a great kingdom south of Israel. The events that both the Old Testament and the New Testament refer to are believed to have taken place around 970 BCE, right in the middle of King Solomon's reign.

Ethiopia has its own unique chronicling of these events in the Kebra Nagast ("The Glory of the Kings"). The Kebra Nagast is basically a rehashing of the events mentioned in the Bible, at least as it pertains to King Solomon's meeting with the Queen of Sheba.

While the biblical account is fairly brief, the Kebra Nagast greatly expands upon it and even suggests that King Solomon had a close relationship with the Queen of Sheba that resulted in her carrying his child. This is, of course, speculation by ancient Ethiopian writers and is beyond the scope of this book to prove. But nevertheless, it must be mentioned because the belief that the Queen of Sheba gave birth to Solomon's son is an integral part of Ethiopian history.

As the Kebra Nagast tells us, the Queen of Sheba returned to her homeland and gave birth to Menelik I, who is said to be King Solomon's son. According to the Kebra Nagast, Menelik I began the so-called Solomonic dynasty, which is said to have lasted all the way until the death of the last Ethiopian monarch, Haile Selassie, in 1975, although there was a brief interruption in the 13th century.

According to this account, Menelik I not only founded the dynasty but also began the practice of Ethiopian Judaism. Although there is no way to verify the Kebra Nagast's claims, Ethiopia does have a history of practicing Judaism, which predates Ethiopia's adoption of Christianity. The Gospels of the New Testament even mention an Ethiopian delegation on a pilgrimage to Israel, indicating that a substantial number of Ethiopians had already converted to Judaism prior to the arrival of Christianity.

Even today, Ethiopia has a substantial Jewish community referred to as Beta Israel; it is primarily located in the northernmost reaches of Ethiopia.

At any rate, if we allow ourselves to entertain the legends found in the Kebra Nagast, the Queen of Sheba gave birth to Solomon's son, Menelik I, who grew up to embrace his Jewish roots. As a young man, he made a return trip to Jerusalem, where his father, Solomon, attempted to convince him to stay in Israel.

Rather than staying, Menelik decided to return home to Ethiopia. But according to the legend, he did not return home empty-handed. The Kebra Nagast insists that Menelik's father Solomon gifted him with none other than the Ark of the Covenant.

The Ark of the Covenant is yet another artifact that is vigorously debated by historians. The Ark, which the Israelites held as sacred, was basically a gold-plated, wooden box with a lid on top and golden rings on its sides. Long poles could be inserted through the rings, allowing the Ark to be carried on the shoulders of priests. At one point, the Ark is said to have carried the stone tablets on which the Ten Commandments were written. According to scripture, the Israelites also believed that the presence and power of God dwelled in the Ark.

Of course, historians would call into question much of the biblical narrative about the Ark of the Covenant, but most agree that some sort of artifact referred to by this name did exist at one time. However, something happened to the Ark, and there is no mention of what happened or where it went. This is where the Kebra Nagast picks up the story, insisting that it was given to Menelik by his father. It was brought back to Ethiopia for safe-keeping. There are Ethiopians to this very day who insist that the Ark is still hidden away somewhere in a secret Ethiopian monastery, where it is carefully guarded by Ethiopian priests.

For the moment, let us move away from the legendary Kebra Nagast. Historians believe that the first true Ethiopian kingdom was D'mt or, as it is sometimes rendered in English, Damot or Da Ma'at. Although the exact date of the kingdom's foundation is unknown, it is widely believed that D'mt began sometime around

1000 BCE. This would place the founding of the kingdom just prior to the Queen of Sheba's visit to Solomon.

The Kingdom of D'mt is located in what used to be northern Ethiopia; today, it exists as part of the breakaway Ethiopian region of Eritrea. Some parts of D'mt were also said to reside in the northern Ethiopian region of Tigray. According to what has been discovered by archaeologists, the residents of D'mt possessed Iron Age instruments, used farm equipment like the plow, and harvested and stockpiled an abundance of grain.

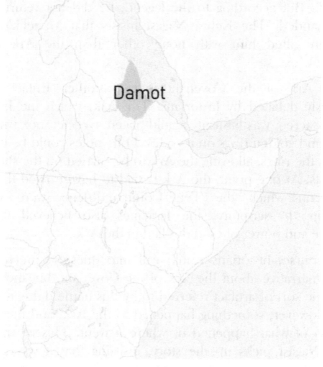

D'mt at its peak.

Due to D'mt's location right at the juncture of the Red Sea, which borders Arabia, it is believed heavy Arabian influence was present. It is thought this influence mainly came from the Sabean civilization of South Arabia (now modern-day Yemen). During D'mt's existence, Semitic language and writing came to prominence. This was the first known Ethiopian script, Ge'ez.

This kingdom thrived until around 500 BCE. Around this time, the archaeological record shows that the old D'mt kingdom was going into decline, becoming dominated by several much smaller successor states. These smaller kingdoms would reign supreme until the rise of the Aksumite Empire sometime around the 1st century CE. This kingdom would come to dominate northern Ethiopia, as it was situated around the modern-day regions of Tigray and Eritrea.

Aksum at its greatest height.

At its height, the Kingdom of Aksum would cross the Arabian Sea and take up root in the southern corner of the Arabian Peninsula in what today constitutes the modern-day nation of Yemen. The capital of the Aksumite Empire was the city that bore the same name—the city of Aksum. This northern Ethiopian city is still in existence to this day and remains quite a tourist attraction, as it has many notable monasteries and monuments still standing.

The Aksumite Empire was well connected at its height, establishing contact and commerce with the outside world primarily through the Red Sea port of Adulis, located in modern-day Eritrea. As an indication of the difficulty of overland travel, it's said that it would often take several days for travelers from the inland city of Aksum to reach the port of Adulis.

A basic overview of trade routes in the 1ˢᵗ century CE.

Nevertheless, Adulis would become the primary trading hub for the Aksumite Ethiopians. The 1st-century Roman historian Pliny the Elder referenced Adulis as being Ethiopia's main trading center. A lot of money passed through this port, and Ethiopian coins with Greek inscriptions can still be found in the region. The reason Greek script is found on these coins is due to the fact that Greek was the most common and widespread language. It was used universally among many nations to help better facilitate trade. Along with trading with the Greco-Roman world, there is evidence that Adulis also received trade even farther afield, namely from Persia and India.

The Aksumite Empire was also successful in war. Around the 3rd century CE, one of the great Aksumite kings—Aphilas—managed to greatly expand the kingdom by launching a successful military expedition over the Red Sea and into southern Arabia. Aphilas's forces successfully subdued the neighboring southern coast of the Arabian Peninsula and extended Ethiopia's reach into Arabia itself.

Ethiopia was a force to be reckoned with in the 3rd century. As a testament to this fact, it was listed as one of the great powers of the world, along with China, Persia, and the Roman Empire itself. This list was compiled by the notable Persian mystic of the Manichean faith, Mani.

Around the 4th century, between 300 and 400 CE, another powerful Aksumite monarch took center stage in Ethiopian affairs. His name comes down to us as Ezana, and many important monuments, such as the famed Ezana Stone, have been inscribed with his name. Ezana is said to be the Ethiopian monarch who approved Ethiopia's official acceptance of Christianity as a state religion around 324 CE.

A picture of the Ezana Stone.

This would make Ethiopia the second nation to formally accept Christianity as its official religion, preceded only by the Kingdom of Armenia, which adopted the Christian faith in 301 CE. Ethiopia beat the Roman Empire in embracing Christianity since the religion was not the official faith of Rome until 380. It is true that Rome was already tolerant of the religion. Back in 313 CE, Roman Emperor Constantine signed edicts that indicated the empire's tolerance toward the religion, but it was not until 380 that Christianity became the official religion of the Roman Empire.

Under Ezana, the Kingdom of Aksum was still in control of a sizeable territory, which stretched right across the Red Sea and into the Arabian Peninsula. It seems that while consolidating these landholdings, Ezana's greatest threats were not from the outside but rather from within. Most of his military engagements were notably against insurgencies within the empire itself. However, there is extensive mention of the Aksumite conquest of the Kingdom of Meroe, which was located on the Upper Nile.

Scholars can see when the empire shifted from widespread pagan beliefs to Christianity. Prior to the conversion, Ezana would have stones inscribed with praises to pagan deities. But after the empire converted to Christianity, stone inscriptions had a Christian flair, with words dedicated to the "Lord of Heaven and Lord of the Earth." After the Christian conversion, the Aksumite Empire's coins began having Christian phrases and the sign of the cross inscribed on them.

Now that we have mentioned the Aksumite Empire's conversion to Christianity, we might as well attempt to understand how this conversion came about. The simplest explanation would probably be the general move toward Christianity, as the religion gained popularity among the general public. But as is often the case in conversion stories, there is a much more dramatic explanation for Ethiopia's sudden emergence into the Christian fold.

It's said that in 316 CE, a Christian missionary from Tyre by the name of Frumentius, his sibling Aedeius, and an unnamed uncle were making a trip to one of Aksum's Red Sea ports when they were ambushed by local Ethiopians. The reason this ambush occurred is not given, but the two brothers, Frumentius and Aedeius, were spared.

As the chronicler of this event put it, "The boys were found studying under a tree and preparing their lessons, and preserved by the mercy of the Barbarians, were taken to the King. He made one of them, Aedeius, his cupbearer. Frumentius, whom he had perceived to be sagacious and prudent, he made his treasurer and secretary. Thereafter they were held in great honor and affection by the King."

According to this chronicler, the two brothers were brought to the Ethiopian king, which at that time was Ezana's predecessor, Ella Amida (also known as Ella Allada or Ousanas). After the king was introduced to the captives, he made them a part of his court. It was supposedly from their royal perch, right in the midst of the king's court, that the two youths managed to spread the Gospel. They also got to know King Ella Amida's son, Ezana.

According to this account, Ezana took the throne with a thorough knowledge of Christianity. Shortly thereafter, he opted to adopt the faith as Ethiopia's national religion. Frumentius would go on to be appointed as the first patriarch of what would become the Ethiopian Orthodox Church. This was apparently done with the blessing of the patriarch of Alexandria, Egypt.

In those days, Egypt was a part of the Roman Empire. Despite Rome's periodic persecutions of Christians, Egypt had long been a refuge for Christians. As such, the Coptic Christians of Alexandria, Egypt, can be considered a mentor and a sort of elder sibling of the faith to the Ethiopians, even though they were one of the first to embrace Christianity as a state religion.

The Kingdom of Aksum expanded and prospered under Ezana's reign, and extensive trade along the famed Silk Road, which stretched through the Roman Empire all the way to China, has been recorded.

Ethiopia traded goods like ivory, gold, emeralds, and even tortoise shells. In exchange, Ethiopia heavily imported China's much-coveted silk (after which the Silk Road was named), as well as a wide variety of spices.

Although so far we have used the term "Ethiopia" fairly interchangeably, it was actually under King Ezana that the term came into widespread use. During the period of international trade and rapid expansion under Ezana, Ethiopia first entered the lexicon and experienced what has been termed a true "golden age."

Chapter 2 – Unrest and Decline in the Kingdom of Aksum

"As Ethiopia goes, so goes the whole Horn of Africa."

-Eskinder Nega

After the fall of the Western Roman Empire, the Ethiopian Kingdom of Aksum was often in flux, as it faced the general turbulence of the times. But even though contact with Rome and the Western Roman Empire had been lost, the eastern half, later known as the Byzantine Empire, would continue to have strong relations with Ethiopia. Byzantine Emperor Justin I, for example, who reigned from 518 to 527, was on close terms with Emperor Kaleb I of Aksum.

In fact, the two Christian empires actually coordinated a joint mission against a local nemesis. Around this point in time, Ethiopia had temporarily lost control of the southwestern portion of Arabia, so the two Christian leaders hatched a plot to get this former Ethiopian territory back under Aksumite control.

This former Ethiopian territory had become part of the Himyarite Kingdom, which was under the leadership of Dhu Nawas. The Himyarite Kingdom had previously converted to Judaism, but due to reports that Himyar was mistreating Christian residents, with some Christian merchants even being killed, both the Byzantines and the Ethiopians began to consider military action against the Himyarite Kingdom.

The Byzantines apparently gave the Ethiopians the go-ahead for military action, and Emperor Kaleb I began issuing warnings and ultimatums to the Himyarite king. In one of his missives, Kaleb I admonished the Himyarites, stating, "You have acted badly because you have killed merchants of the Christian Romans, which is a loss both to myself and my kingdom."

Here, it seems that Kaleb is speaking about a commercial loss as much as he might be invoking a moral loss. Ethiopia depended on trade with the Eastern Roman Empire, and the slaughter of Roman merchants hit the Ethiopians where it hurt—their pocketbook! So, the Ethiopians hooked up with the Byzantine Greeks. In 524, they used Greek ships to ferry their troops across the Red Sea to wage war against the Himyarite Kingdom. Kaleb's forces were successful in toppling the Himyarite regime, reasserting Ethiopian control over southwest Arabia.

At one point, Kaleb even attempted to extend his reach all the way to Mecca. To be clear, this incident occurred some one hundred years before the rise of Islam, but by the time of Muhammad, it was still remembered. The occasion was even briefly mentioned in the Quran.

In between Kaleb's invasion and the rise of Islam in Arabia, the balance of power in southwestern Arabia (Yemen) would shift back and forth between Ethiopia and Persia. The two main powers of the region were the Byzantine Empire and the Persian Empire. Even while fighting the Ethiopians, the Persians were skirmishing with the Byzantines. The Arabian front against the Aksumites was just one theater of this multi-front war.

After the Byzantines and Persians basically fought to a standstill, both parties and their proxies (such as the Byzantine Empire's proxy of Ethiopia) were taken completely off-guard by the sudden rise of Islam in Arabia. Ethiopia had an interesting card to play in all of this. Before Islam managed to unite the Arab tribes and take over the Arabian Peninsula, the Aksumite king, Armah, gave refuge to early Muslim believers when they were still a persecuted sect in Arabia. These actions were remembered when Islam took over the Arabian Peninsula. This seems to have stayed Muhammad's hand as it pertained to Ethiopia. During Muhammad's lifetime, the Muslims' early battles were aimed at Byzantine and Persian territory. They noticeably avoided a quick trip across the Red Sea to subdue neighboring Ethiopia.

But this was just a brief reprieve. Not long after Muhammad's death in 632, his successors began to turn their attention toward Ethiopia. Sometime in the 700s, Muslim forces stormed one of Ethiopia's established ports on the Red Sea, destroying it. The Ethiopians would never regain this trading hub, and from this point on, Ethiopia would contract increasingly inward. Meanwhile, the forces of Islam, which had swept across all of North Africa and were encroaching on Africa's Eastern Horn, began to steadily surround the Ethiopian kingdom.

Internal discord also came to play a role in further shrinking the Aksumite Empire. And as the internal discord grew, a troubling new leader rose to the Aksumite throne, threatening to undo everything her predecessors had achieved. Her name comes down to us as Judith or, as it is rendered in the Amharic vernacular, "Gudit." She is also recalled with popular disdain, as she is nicknamed "Yodit Gudit," which is a smart corruption of her name. It basically means "Evil Gudit."

Gudit (Judith) is remembered as being evil because she not only managed to topple the Aksumite Empire but also attempted to topple the already long-established tradition of Christianity. Her full backstory is not entirely clear, but what is often repeated is that she somehow rose to power, had the rightful Ethiopian king overthrown and killed, and then crowned herself queen. Since she reigned for a whopping forty-some years, it is indeed rather astonishing that not a whole lot more is known about this long-lived Ethiopian monarch.

Yet, even though some of the more exact details are sparse, Yodit Gudit is a common trope in Ethiopian folklore to this very day. But why was she evil? Well, besides overthrowing her predecessor, she seems to have had a bent toward paganism and wished to somehow roll back the clock to take the majority of the population back to the pre-Christian era so paganism could flourish. Since most Ethiopians firmly embraced Orthodox Christianity by this point, it was a losing battle, even for an iron-willed, authoritarian dictator like Gudit.

Nevertheless, she began a campaign of terror in which she killed Christians and burned down churches and holy shrines. Gudit is credited with destroying a large chunk of Aksum's ancient monuments. Gudit is also remembered for moving the capital from Aksum to somewhere farther south, in the vicinity of what would eventually become the famed city of Lalibela.

The move toward a more centralized capital would continue for several centuries. As the years progressed and as Ethiopia marched inward, the Red Sea would increasingly be seen as the stomping ground of Ethiopia's enemies rather than a resource that Ethiopians would be able to use.

Many view Gudit's decision to move farther into the Ethiopian interior as the first step in this process. After Gudit's demise, a new dynasty, the Zagwe dynasty, would take root and make Lalibela their permanent capital. The Zagwe dynasty, which would ultimately span from 912 to 1137, spent much of its time seeking to undo the damage that had been wrought by Queen Gudit.

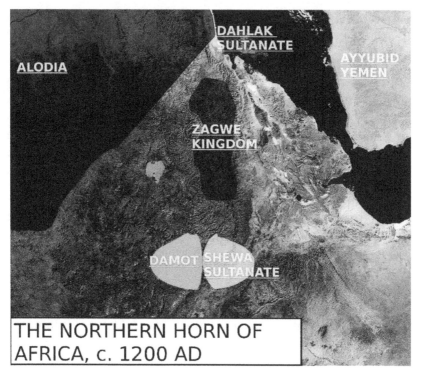

A map of Zagwe circa 1200.

One of the first things the Zagwe dynasty did was reestablish ties with the Patriarchate of Alexandria. Egypt had been taken over by Muslim armies during the first great wave of Islamic conquest that took over the whole of North Africa. Nevertheless, a sizeable Christian Orthodox community commonly known as the Copts would remain in place, albeit under Islamic rule. The Ethiopians, whose own Orthodox church had been approved by the Patriarchate of Alexandria back in the 4th century, still viewed the Patriarchate of Alexandria as their mother church.

Due to the everyday realities of Egypt's occupation by Muslim forces, communication between Ethiopian Orthodox churches and Egyptian Orthodox churches had become greatly strained. This delayed correspondence ultimately delayed the Alexandrian patriarch's ability to sanction the placement of a new archbishop in Ethiopia. If the Muslim rulers wished, they could block all communication between the two churches entirely.

But fortunately for the Zagwe dynasty, Egypt's overlords allowed a tenuous strand of contact between the two Orthodox churches. Scholar and Ethiopian historian David Buxton has something rather interesting to say about this. He posits there is an added element to this relationship that other historians might miss.

According to Buxton, there was a long-standing superstitious fear held by the rulers of Egypt. They believed that the kings of Ethiopia had control over the Nile River. The Nile, which actually begins in Ethiopia and then flows north into Egypt and ultimately out into the Mediterranean, had long been the lifeblood of the Egyptians. Without the replenishment of the Nile's waters, the desert-like environment of Egypt would not be able to prosper. Buxton insists that it was this deep-seated fear of Ethiopians somehow tampering with the Nile and causing Egypt to run dry that might have led to a more cautious approach when it came to Egyptian rulers dealing with Ethiopia.

Buxton contends that Ethiopians were also aware of this. Through the centuries, various Ethiopian kings have made threats to somehow "divert the Nile" when faced with poor treatment by Egypt. It is fascinating that Buxton points this out because, in the 21st century, one of the greatest flashpoints and conflicts in the entire African continent is between Egypt and Ethiopia. And it is over the Nile River.

Starting in 2011, Ethiopia began work on a hydroelectric dam at the base of the Nile in a bid to produce more energy for the nation. But Egypt voiced concerns over the project from the very beginning, worrying that Ethiopia would end up draining the Nile with its dam, causing Egypt to go dry. The dam project has been underway for several years, and despite efforts to mediate a solution, it has repeatedly caused conflict. With the filling of the dam in 2020, 2021, and 2022, threats and bitter recriminations have been hurled back and forth between the two nations. We are getting a bit ahead of ourselves here in Ethiopian history, but it really is quite astonishing to see how long this fear (whether it is merited or not) of Ethiopians controlling the Nile has been a part of the Egyptian psyche.

At any rate, the Zagwe kings were able to expand Ethiopian territory for the first time in centuries. However, most of their territorial gains were in mountainous regions with exceedingly rough terrain, and their ability to actually control these wild, untamed lands is debatable. At any rate, the Zagwe dynasty attempted to exert control over all of modern-day Eritrea to the north and on down to Wollo Province in the south. They even marched all the way to Ethiopia's Lake Tana in the west. Lake Tana is the repository of the so-called "Blue Nile." This region was of great strategic importance since controlling the Blue Nile gave Ethiopians a perceived upper hand over their Egyptian neighbors in the north.

Along with securing strategic outposts at home, the Zagwe dynasty also sent Ethiopians abroad, in particular, on pilgrimages to Jerusalem. In 1189, an Ethiopian delegation arrived in Israel and met up with the Muslim leader Saladin, who was in control of Jerusalem.

To the Ethiopians of this time period, pilgrimages to Jerusalem were of tremendous importance, and frequent pilgrimages were carried out. As a result of the Crusades, Jerusalem was under Christian control from 1099 to 1187. After Jerusalem fell to Islamic forces in 1187, Ethiopian King Lalibela became inspired to build his own sacred pilgrimage site within Ethiopia itself.

King Lalibela figured that if his people could not reach the Holy Land, he would simply create a replica within his own borders. King Lalibela sought to create a "New Jerusalem," if you will, in the capital city that would ultimately bear his name. This meant that the local river that flowed through the city would be renamed "Jordan," just like the Jordan River in Israel. There would be several other name changes to common features in the local environment.

But most spectacular are the eleven huge stone churches that were hewn right out of solid rock. According to Ethiopian legend, these churches were supernaturally constructed by angels. Since there is no other historical reference to how these stunning monasteries were built, the idea of angelic intervention does indeed remain the preferred explanation.

Even though the Zagwe kings were later viewed as usurpers since they were not from the Solomonic dynasty, Lalibela is generally revered by Ethiopian chroniclers for his efforts. Lalibela's successor Yetbarak would become the last and final ruler of the Zagwe dynasty.

Some accounts point to a figure who immediately preceded Yetbarak, Na'akueto La'ab, as being the last of the Zagwe rulers. These accounts apparently do not recognize Yetbarak's legitimacy. But according to most variations, Na'akueto La'ab's rule was brief, and after some infighting, he was replaced by Yetbarak, which made him the last Zagwe king. At any rate, it is said that Yetbarak ultimately waged war against Yekuno Amlak, a so-called "Amhara nobleman" who claimed descent from the Solomonic line.

Not a whole lot is known about how this played out, but the last Zagwe king, Yetbarak, perished in battle, and Yekuno Amlak was ultimately successful in reestablishing the Solomonic line, with himself as the first king of the restored order. With the restoration of the Solomonic dynasty, the medieval period of Ethiopia's growth and expansion began.

Chapter 3 – Solomonic Dynasty Restored

"Wake up Ethiopia! Wake up Africa! Let us work towards the one glorious end of a free, redeemed and mighty nation. Let Africa be a bright star among the constellation of nations."

-Marcus Garvey

Not a whole lot is known about Ethiopia during the early days of the Solomonic dynasty's restoration. But shortly after the reestablishment (although some might say establishment) of this dynastic line, in the early 1300s, the medieval Ethiopian text known as the Kebra Nagast first appeared. For those who do not wish to believe in the legend this book presents of Ethiopian kings tracing themselves back to a union between the Queen of Sheba and King Solomon, it could be argued that the sudden appearance of the Kebra Nagast was nothing more than a convenient propaganda piece.

Again, this writer is not taking a side either way but rather pointing out the different perspectives that could be formulated. It certainly could be considered convenient because it was right on the heels of the supposed reestablishment of the Solomonic line that Kebra Nagast's compilation was sanctioned. It served as a written legitimatization of the Solomonic dynasty's rule.

At any rate, of what we know of the later Solomonic kings of this period, one who stands out is a figure known as Amda Tsion I (also spelled as Amda Seyon). Amda began his reign in scandal. It was said that he was a young, highly immoral king who seemed to enjoy raucous parties more than statecraft, so much so that he was openly rebuked by Ethiopian priests. Regardless, Amda grew into the role he was given, and when the kingdom was rocked by some of the earliest incursions by neighboring Islamic powers, King Amda stood up to the threat and decisively thwarted Islamic expansion into Ethiopia.

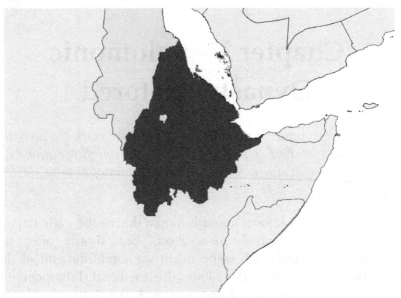

Ethiopian Empire after Amda Tsion's conquests.

Amda's name was praised for his heroism in battle, and many local songs were crafted in his honor. Still, the threat of being engulfed by the Islamic nations that surrounded Ethiopia persisted. And by the early 1400s, the Ethiopian leadership finally began to look elsewhere for a potential lifeline of support before the state was swallowed up completely. It was with this in mind that Ethiopian King Yeshaq I fired off a missive to the Spanish king, Alfonso V of Aragon, in 1428.

At the time, Spain was fighting a bloody Reconquista to take back territory that had been conquered by Islamic forces. The Spanish king fully understood the danger that Ethiopia was in. King Alfonso was moved enough by Yeshaq's calls for help that he immediately sent a delegation to Ethiopia. Needless to say, the journey from Spain to Ethiopia was a treacherous run, one that required traveling through hostile territories.

And although Alfonso sent out this delegation to speak with the Ethiopians, it remains a mystery what happened to them. The delegation never returned to Spain, and it remains unclear if they even managed to reach Ethiopia. Toward the end of Alfonso's reign, he tried to reach out to Ethiopia once again, sending a message to Ethiopian Emperor Zara Yaqob in 1450, but again, his entreaties failed to reach the Ethiopian court.

Zara Yaqob, also dubbed Kwestantinos (as in the Roman Constantine), was himself an interesting figure in Ethiopian history. He has been compared with the likes of later Ethiopian greats like Menelik II and even the last and final Ethiopian emperor, Haile Selassie. Zara Yaqob was known to be a fierce defender of the faith and was successful in pushing back outside threats to the kingdom.

Most notably, at the Battle of Gomit in 1445, Zara Yaqob led an army against Sultan Badlay ibn Sa'ad ad-Din, who controlled a sultanate in the Adal region of the Horn of Africa. Emperor Zara Yaqob was able to soundly defeat the sultan's forces, eliminating the latest threat to Ethiopian sovereignty.

Zara Yaqob is also known for founding another Ethiopian capital, this one located in central Ethiopia in Debre Birhan. It has been said that the king was inspired to found his new capital at this location after he bore witness to some sort of unidentified bright light flying across the sky. Today, it has been widely speculated that this unidentified object was likely Haley's Comet, but in truth, no one really knows for sure. Whatever it was, Yaqob, like most people of his day and age, ascribed the sight to be a divine sign.

Although Yaqob is remembered for his heroic deeds, he also went down in history as being a bit of a despot, as he was more than willing to use oppression to control his people. He employed a heavy hand with the Ethiopian Orthodox Church, directly interfering with the internal happenings of Ethiopian clergy as he saw fit. Times were tough for Ethiopia, and rulers like Yaqob thought that an iron first was needed to quell both external and internal threats.

By the early 1500s, external threats would once again take center stage. The Adal Sultanate in the eastern Horn of Africa, roughly located in and around modern-day Somalia, began to make even more aggressive inroads into Ethiopian territory. Around this time, Lebna Dengel rose to the Ethiopian throne. Upon gaining the crown, Dengel was dubbed Dawit II (as in King David of the Bible). Dawit II, like his predecessors, would face the threat of Islamic incursions in Ethiopia's borderlands.

Lebna Dengel.

During Dawit II's early reign, he sought to negotiate peaceful settlements with local antagonists, but when this did not work, the young king was forced to go to war. He managed to score some early victories. For instance, in 1517, he led a force of troops that managed to take out the emir of Adal, Mahfuz.

During this time, some very interesting reports were coming in describing mysterious strangers who laid siege to the nearby Islamic fortress at Zeila on the East African coast. These mysterious strangers were Portuguese explorers. They were the first Europeans to successfully round the tip of Africa and make their presence felt in the Red Sea.

The Portuguese actually had two goals in mind at the time. They wanted to reestablish contact with India (direct trade with India had been lost after the fall of Constantinople in 1453), and they were in search of a legendary Christian king located somewhere in the East. This man, Prester John, had been cut off from the rest of Christendom, and the Portuguese wished to reconnect with him. Some thought this Christian king was in India, but others came to believe that this mysterious lost Christian kingdom was located in none other than Ethiopia.

At any rate, the Portuguese soon came into conflict with local Muslim sultans, and as fate would have it, the European explorers began waging war against them just as Ethiopian Emperor Dawit II was struggling against them. The Portuguese eventually made contact with Dawit II, and preliminary diplomatic relations between Portugal and Ethiopia began in earnest.

Ethiopia would face a dire existential threat to its existence in 1528. A new sultan by the name of Ahmad ibn Ibrahim al-Ghazi unleashed an all-out war against Ethiopia. That fateful year, the sultan led his forces across the Awash River and began to devastate the city of Bedeque. Dawit II and his troops arrived on the scene, and the sultan's army made a tactical retreat.

The two sides would again clash in the spring of 1529. This time, the Ethiopian army would be dealt a terrible setback and face a decisive defeat. Emboldened, the sultan continued to hammer at the Ethiopian army over the next few years. Unable to handle a sustained assault, which included the sultan's use of an early form of artillery, Ethiopian Emperor Dawit II reached out to the Portuguese for help.

At this point, Dawit II had become little more than a fugitive in his own kingdom. Dawit II and what was left of the Ethiopian resistance were forced to move from one embattled encampment to the next as they were mercilessly hounded by their opponents. Emperor Dawit II would ultimately perish before the Portuguese could arrive. Nevertheless, right when the Ethiopian cause seemed absolutely hopeless, what must have seemed like a miracle to the beleaguered Ethiopian citizens took place.

In the fall of 1540, around four hundred Portuguese troops arrived on the scene and galvanized what was left of the Ethiopian resistance. Together, they smashed right into the sultan's forces. This combined force was led by none other than Christopher da Gama, the son of famed Portuguese explorer Vasco da Gama. Christopher da Gama fought hard against his opponents. He ultimately lost his life in the Battle of Wofla in 1542.

Nevertheless, the Portuguese and Ethiopians continued the fight, and the sultanate was defeated, allowing Dawit II's successor, Gelawdewos, to be able to rule in peace. According to Ethiopian historian David Buxton, the Portuguese veterans of the Ethiopian-Adal War were viewed with tremendous respect for their efforts. Gelawdewos described the Portuguese fighters as being "powerful and valorous men athirst for war like wolves and hungry for the fight like lions."

If it wasn't for the arrival of these few hundred Portuguese troops, men already well-versed in bloody warfare, the Ethiopian civilization may well have been extinguished. These men gave everything they had to defend Ethiopia, and according to Buxton, most of them decided to stay on as guardians of this Christian kingdom. According to Buxton, "[The Portuguese] were held in great respect, married high-born local ladies, and gradually merged with the Abyssinian population."

But as much as the Portuguese helped the Ethiopians stave off disaster, the subsequent relations between Ethiopia and Portugal were not always smooth. This was due to the religious differences between Ethiopian Orthodox and Portuguese Catholicism. Sure, they were both Christians, but once one digs deeper into their doctrines, problems inevitably arise. And during a time when one's doctrine meant just about everything, such things could be quite troubling.

After aiding Ethiopia, Portugal naturally wanted to establish Catholic missions in the African nation. The Ethiopian Orthodox Church obviously did not want their faithful to be purloined by the Catholic Church. Yet, in light of the tremendous aid that Portugal had given Ethiopia, Ethiopian monarchs initially felt obligated to appease the Catholics. This appeasement continued for nearly one hundred years and came to a head in the early 1600s when Ethiopian Emperor Susenyos was actually convinced by Portuguese Jesuit priests to convert to Catholicism.

The Portuguese no doubt rejoiced at the thought that all of Ethiopia was about to enter the Catholic fold. But they underestimated how deep the roots of Ethiopia's Orthodox Church were. Emperor Susenyos's conversion created so much tumult that rather than converting his nation, he was forced out of office. As soon as the church and the lower classes of Ethiopian society heard of Susenyos's intentions, they rose up in revolt and very nearly sparked a civil war.

This pressure caused the newly converted Catholic king to step down so that his son Fasilides (or Fasil) could rule in his stead. Considering all of the drama that had erupted under his father's watch, Emperor Fasilides issued a decree that sent the Catholic Jesuits back to Portugal. This series of events ended official efforts to convert Ethiopians to Catholicism.

Along with expelling the Jesuits, Emperor Fasilides also founded another new Ethiopian capital, establishing Gondar in 1636. Here, he built impressive castles, churches, and other monuments that still stand to this day.

Fasilides Palace in Gondar.

According to Ethiopian scholar Bahru Zewde, major demographic changes happened during this period. According to Zewde, at the end of the Ethiopian-Adal War, Ethiopia experienced a massive influx of Oromo people from the highlands. This is important to note since the Oromo would eventually come to represent a large chunk of the Ethiopian population. This influx of newcomers would lead to great tensions and even sporadic warfare.

In this backdrop of instability, a rapid succession of kings took place throughout much of the rest of the 17th century. And the 1700s were not much better. The situation was so unstable that, at one point, an Ethiopian emperor by the name of Iyasu I was actually killed by his own son, Tekle Haymanot. Tekle Haymanot would be assassinated shortly thereafter. Several years of similar turbulence ensued. The year 1769 was a watershed moment in Ethiopian history; it marked the final centralized Ethiopian leader of this period to attempt to reassert control out of the chaos the country found itself in.

Ethiopian Emperor Iyoas attempted to regain control of the situation from his perch in Gondor, only to be assassinated by the governor of nearby Tigray Province, Ras Mikael Sehul. It's worth noting that "Ras" is an Amharic word for "governor." For example, Emperor Haile Selassie, whose birth name was Tafari, was once a governor or Ras and was thus known as Ras Tafari. This title would inspire the later Rastafarian movement in Jamaica, as they had come to idolize Haile Selassie.

At any rate, after Ras Mikael Sehul, the governor of Tigray, murdered Ethiopian Emperor Iyoas in 1769, Ethiopia entered a period known as the Zemene Mesafint or, as it is rendered in English, the "Era of the Princes."

Chapter 4 – The Era of the Princes and the Rise of Tewodros II

"I know their game. First, the traders and the missionaries—then the ambassadors; then the cannon. It's better to go straight to the cannon."

-Tewodros II

The year 1769 is generally known as a watershed moment in Ethiopian history. This era is called the Era of the Princes because a series of governors, princes, and other notables would spend several decades being the true power behind the Ethiopian throne. The start of this epoch was witnessed by an outside observer: Scottish explorer and scholar James Bruce.

Bruce is perhaps most famous for retrieving a copy of the lost Book of Enoch from an Ethiopian monastery. But his presence during this pivotal point in Ethiopian history provides some valuable insight into Ethiopia's political strife. Bruce saw what seemed to be a complete breakdown of society, caused by a revolving door of Ethiopian emperors whose strings were being pulled by various members of the Ethiopian nobility.

First, Ras Mikael Sehul assassinated Iyoas I (sometimes spelled Joas), the reigning emperor, and installed his own crony, Yohannes II. This would begin the Era of the Princes, during which a succession of weak puppet emperors was put in place by scheming nobles or "princes" in their own bid to control Ethiopia. As it pertains to the manipulated reign of Yohannes II, he managed to get on his benefactor's bad side and was removed from power. Some accounts state that he was put to death.

After Yohannes II was deposed, Ras Mikael Sehul engineered the installment of his young son Tekle Haymanot II, who was only around fifteen years old at the time. It was around the time that Tekle Haymanot II was installed on the throne that Scottish explorer James Bruce entered the picture. Bruce gave a vivid description of the new Ethiopian emperor, stating, "He had an excellent understanding, and prudence beyond his years. He was said to be naturally of a very warm temper, but this he had so perfectly subdued, as scarcely ever to have given an instance of it in public. He entered into Ras Mikael's views entirely, and was as forward to march out against Fasil, as his father had been averse to it."

In these remarks, Bruce makes reference to the leading noble of the Ethiopian court: "Ras Mikael." Bruce realized that Mikael was the one pulling the strings since the young new emperor was beholden to "Ras Mikael's views entirely." Indeed, Tekle Haymanot II's very right to sit on the throne was beholden to Ras Mikael. This was demonstrated in 1770, shortly after his installment. That fateful year, Ras Mikael was forced to leave Gondar to attend to business elsewhere. While he was away, his opponents struck.

Tekle Haymanot II was deposed by a rival faction in the city, which installed a new emperor, Susenyos II. Once Ras Mikael returned, Tekle Haymanot II was reinstalled. This, of course, was no easy feat, and once Ras Mikael regained the upper hand in the struggle, there was hell to pay.

Ras Mikael instituted a reign of terror, rooting out his rivals and all who supported them. Once again, we get a firsthand account of how these things played out from Scottish explorer James Bruce.

Bruce tells us, "The bodies of those killed by the sword were hewn to pieces and scattered about the streets, being denied burial. I was miserable, and almost driven to despair, at seeing my hunting dogs, twice let loose by the carelessness of my servants, bringing into the courtyard the head and arms of killed men. The quantity of carrion, and the stench of it, brought down the hyaenas in hundreds from the neighboring mountains; and, as few people in Gondar go out after dark, they enjoyed the streets to themselves, and seemed ready to dispute the possession of the city with the inhabitants."

It is quite gripping to imagine James Bruce, sitting in his courtyard, perhaps even studying copies of the legendary Book of Enoch, to look up and see one of his dogs munching on the retrieved arm of one of Ras Mikael's victims. Ras Mikael's reign of terror was stopped when a coalition of his opponents defeated him in battle in June 1771. He was then taken into the custody of another leading Ethiopian "prince," Wand Bewossen, the governor of Lasta.

However, the victors of this struggle were surprisingly lenient with Ras Mikael. After being confined for a year, he was actually reinstalled as the governor of Tigray. Wand Bewossen was bested in 1772 by yet another assortment of "princes" and made to return to his post as governor of Lasta.

Emperor Tekle Haymanot II would remain on the throne during all of this infighting, relatively helpless to control or stop any of it. He ultimately abdicated in 1777 and opted to live the rest of his life in exile, studying the scriptures. In his place, leading Ethiopian figures installed Emperor Salomon II. Salomon II, who largely served the interests of the Ethiopian nobility, was forced out of office in 1779. Just like his predecessor, he lived the rest of his life like a monk. Tekle Haymanot II's brother, Tekle Giyorgis, was put on the throne next; his reign would last until 1800.

Later, another "kingmaker" would arise in Ethiopia: Ras Walda-Sellasse (also spelled as Wolde Selassie). Ras Walda-Sellasse famously made the acquaintance of British writer and explorer Henry Salt, who had an audience with Walda-Sellasse in 1805. Salt erroneously described Ras Walda-Sellasse as the "prime minister" of Ethiopia. Yet, considering the situation, it is understandable why Salt would perceive Ras Walda-Sellasse as such. A "prince" or "Ras," such as Walda-Sellasse, would often serve as the direct intermediary for the king, as would be the case in Britain's own constitutional monarchy.

This turbulent period of instability came to an end in 1855 when a powerful monarch who called himself Tewodros II came to the throne. In many ways, Tewodros (his birth name was Kasa Haylu or Kassa Hailu) was ahead of his time. He realized the need for a strong centralized Ethiopian government and a universal Ethiopian identity.

He also understood the plight of the peasant class, who were largely relegated to farming and manual labor. The peasants often suffered the most during the long instability of the Era of the Princes since they were forced to be subject to the warring nobility's whims. They had to offer up their fresh harvested crops and even their homes if one of the warring nobles requested their aid. This hospitality was often completely at the peasants' expense, and if they were discovered to be holding out on the elites when sustenance was demanded of them, the consequences could be dire.

Yet another British visitor to Ethiopia—one Mansfield Parkyns—supposedly bore witness to such an incident. During a military campaign, Ethiopian soldiers lodged at the home of a local peasant family. It was learned that the owner of the house had secretly hidden some butter from the troops. For this offense, the peasant was said to have been "roasted alive." So, yes, for the common peasant farmer forced to deal with droughts, locusts, and soldiers living under their own roof, life was very hard. Tewodros understood this well.

Although Tewodros was linked to the nobility through his relation to Ethiopian noble and chief figure of the Era of the Princes Dajjacj Maru of Dambya, he was an unlikely figure to rise to the top of the Ethiopian hierarchy. Tewodros grew up in the town of Qawra on the Sudanese-Ethiopian border. This was a dangerous frontier country at the time, with Egyptian troops roving the borderlands.

In order to understand the situation, a bit of background is necessary. As mentioned earlier, the once predominantly Christian Egypt was toppled in the first major wave of Islamic conquest in the 7th century. Egypt then passed between various Islamic power brokers, such as the Abbasids, Fatimids, Ayyubids, and the Mamluks.

In 1517, however, the Ottoman Empire, which was based out of modern-day Turkey, seized control of Egypt and incorporated it into its vast landholdings. By 1805, Egypt was being run by an Ottoman viceroy, Muhammad Ali Pasha. From here on out, Egypt would retain a semi-autonomous status, primarily controlled by Muhammad Ali himself. Under Muhammad Ali, Egypt expanded its reach by taking over a large chunk of Sudan, thereby placing Egyptian troops right on Ethiopia's border. Muhammad Ali Pasha's role was eventually succeeded by his grandson Ishmael in 1863. He would play a role in later conflicts between Egypt and Ethiopia.

Since Tewodros grew up near the Ethiopian-Sudanese border, where the threat of an Egyptian invasion loomed large, he knew just how delicate Ethiopia's security situation really was.

Tewodros also knew what it was like to be poor and to struggle. Although he hailed from nobility (he later claimed his father was distantly related to Emperor Fasilides), he found himself in poverty as a young man, disconnected and disinherited. After his father Haile Giorgis Wolde Giorgis died, it was said that his grandparents, who held a grudge against Tewodros's mother, Woizero Atitegeb Wondbewossen, refused to leave anything to either their daughter-in-law or their grandson.

Upon reaching adulthood, Tewodros resorted to banditry for survival. He became a kind of "Robin Hood" like figure, as he would lead raiding parties against rich targets and then give some of the proceeds to the poor. After Tewodros and his rebels gained a large following, he was able to take his father's inheritance in Qawra by force. Once he had control of the region, he proved himself an able and popular leader who looked out for the common people.

Tewodros's stewardship was so impressive that Empress Menen granted him control of the region Ye Meru Qemas. She also offered him the hand of one of her granddaughters, Tewabech Ali. Tewodros was eager to marry into royalty and accepted the offer. However, his relationship with his mother-in-law would deteriorate. Soon, he would be fielding armies against troops sent by the empress. Nevertheless, Tewodros proved to be too formidable and used his army to topple Empress Menen's husband, Johannes III.

Shortly thereafter, Tewodros was made emperor of Ethiopia in the spring of 1855. This event marked the end of the Era of the Princes and the beginning of a new reign of emperors struggling to establish centralized control over all of Ethiopia.

In many ways, after one hundred years of virtually non-stop infighting and turbulence, it was as if Tewodros had woken Ethiopia up from a long sleeping spell. Ethiopia no longer focused inward; instead, it began to look outward toward the rest of the world.

Tewodros knew there was much work to do. With Egyptian troops encroaching on Ethiopia's borders with the latest artillery, Tewodros's first goal was to modernize the Ethiopian army. Tewodros had a two-fold strategy that consisted of creating a better, more disciplined army and providing the army with modern armaments. As it pertained to improving the discipline and cohesion of Ethiopia's armed forces, Tewodros was marginally successful. In many ways, he was well ahead of his time. And unlike many of his predecessors, he fully understood the need for Ethiopia to have a strong, unified national army.

Rather than having several regional militias to call upon to face external threats, Tewodros realized that Ethiopia needed a unified national force. The Era of the Princes fully demonstrated the weakness of a decentralized army. Regional militias could not always be depended upon when faced with an external threat, and half of the time, they were more likely to fight each other rather than present a unified force.

Tewodros knew that if he was going to quell the Egyptians or any other external threat, he would need a unified national army composed of troops from all sectors of Ethiopia. Of course, realizing such a thing and achieving it are two different things. Tewodros did make some great strides in military reform and deserves credit for that. In particular, Tewodros was the one who began paying his troops regular salaries. He also insisted that soldiers cease the terrible practice of billeting, in which troops could force their way into a home and seize food and whatever other goods they needed from local farmers.

Under Tewodros, the peasants could breathe a little easier knowing that his soldiers were already being paid and would not come around knocking on their doors begging (or demanding) food. However, Tewodros was willing to make some exceptions. In at least one infamous incident, Tewodros allowed looting as a form of reprisal.

Rebel militias in the region of Wollo (also sometimes referred to as Wallo) ambushed one of Tewodros's outposts in the middle of the night. In the melee, Tewodros's own personal guard was killed, and the bandits took off with several mules. Tewodros was so angered by this incident that he sent his troops into the town where these marauders were said to have hailed from and ordered them to exact wholesale looting on the village as a form of collective punishment.

The worst of Tewodros's wrath was reserved for his troops who dared to defy him. There was a reported instance of mutiny shortly after the Wollo incident in which some of his soldiers attempted to rebel.

It has been said that there was a rumor afoot that Tewodros had gone crazy and was planning to launch a Crusade into the Holy Land to reclaim Jerusalem. It sounds a bit absurd for this 19th-century Ethiopian monarch to consider such a thing, but Tewodros, as forward-thinking as he was in certain areas, had his mind stuck back in the days of the Crusades. As we will see, the biggest frustration he developed with the British was the fact they sided with Egyptian Muslims over Ethiopian Christians.

Tewodros did indeed see himself as a kind of crusader and champion of the Christian faith. But having said that, there is no way of knowing whether the gossip among his rebellious soldiers was real or imagined. At any rate, several troops were speaking of Tewodros's supposed plans to march on Jerusalem and convinced a large chunk of his army to mutiny. Tewodros quickly and decisively put down this revolt. It was said that forty-eight of the rebels were hacked to death or shot. According to Ethiopian scholar and historian Bahru Zewde, the two main conspirators of the revolt had their arms and legs hacked off before they were strangled to death by hanging.

Tewodros sought to instill discipline in his ranks with an iron fist, and for a time, his terror tactics worked. But as any totalitarian leader might come to find out, loyalty through fear is no substitution for loyalty out of love. And no matter how much Tewodros cracked down on his soldiers, there would always be a large contingent of his army ready to desert him as soon as the opportunity arose.

Nevertheless, Tewodros did what he thought was best: modernize his armed forces. The other crucial aspect of that was the need for modern armaments. As mentioned, Egyptian troops were encroaching on Ethiopia's borders at the time. And even though their artillery was not as advanced as some other nations, such as the British, their arms still gave them a decisive edge over the Ethiopians, which at that time had very limited armaments.

Tewodros was keenly aware of that fact and began to actively seek European support to build up Ethiopia's arms. In particular, he reached out to Queen Victoria of Britain, requesting technical advisors be sent to Ethiopia to help train Ethiopians at local foundries to craft arms. Again, showing his forward-thinking nature, Tewodros knew that rather than buy guns from foreign nations, it would be best to have Ethiopians trained in gun manufacturing so that they could be built at home.

After Tewodros was shut out by the British government, he began to look in an unusual place for arms development: European missionaries. Ironically enough, missionaries who had arrived in Ethiopia to preach about love and peace were soon being sought after by Tewodros for any potential technical skills they might possess in helping him develop his arsenal.

In the first phase of this outreach, he helped the missionaries set up a technical training school in the town of Gafat. It remains a bit unclear what these missionaries thought they were taking part in, but the school was primarily focused on teaching impoverished youths to read. There were some aspects of technical training, though. Initially, this training was in practical trades, such as masonry. But after continued pressure from Tewodros, those among the missionaries with a little more technical knowledge as it pertained to guns and gunpowder began producing some weapons for the emperor. It is hard telling what the quality of these weapons actually was, but they were apparently functional.

Beyond all odds, Tewodros was making some progress, even though much more needed to be done in order to bring Ethiopia's armaments to the same level as Egypt. In the meantime, Tewodros developed some rather serious enemies within his country. Due to his reforms, he managed to pick a fight with the Ethiopian Orthodox Church.

First, he struck a nerve over something seemingly trivial that was still quite important to the Ethiopian clergy. He began insisting that Ethiopian priests cease wearing their lemiem in front of him. The lemiem is a turban-styled hat that Ethiopian Orthodox priests wear. Tewodros, perhaps showing his stubbornness, was incensed that the priests were the only ones who refused to remove their hats in his presence. But after he forcibly insisted that priests take off their hats, he needlessly provoked a powerful backlash against his rule.

Matters grew even worse when Tewodros began to not only force the Ethiopian Orthodox Church to dispense with their headgear but also with their land. Tewodros was of the opinion that the church had swallowed up too much land and that some of it should be divvied up and given to the peasants. This was a big mistake since the Ethiopian Orthodox Church was the greatest internal power in Ethiopia that could stand against him.

Nevertheless, when questioned about his actions in 1856 by representatives of the church, Tewodros is said to have remarked, "What shall I eat, and with what shall I feed my troops? You have taken half the land as masqual maret, and the other half as rim and gadam." The words masqual maret, rim, and gadam are Ethiopian terms for special distinctions of church property. Tewodros basically said that the Ethiopian Orthodox Church controlled about half of all of Ethiopia through their extensive landholdings. Despite the church's grumbling, Tewodros was not going to back down.

He even tried to assert his authority against visiting representatives of the Egyptian Orthodox Church. The situation in Egypt was already complicated since Tewodros viewed encroachments by the Egyptian army as a threat, even though the Egyptian Orthodox Church represented a large minority of the Egyptian population.

Things came to a head in 1857 when Tewodros apparently became convinced that Coptic priests were engaging in espionage. He had Coptic Patriarch Kyrillos Makarios (Cyrillus Macaire) arrested. Tewodros's stringent measures with his military and the oppression of the church tanked his popularity. Slowly but surely, his troops began to defect and join rebel groups. His army had once numbered around sixty thousand, but it was eventually reduced to ten thousand.

Even though Tewodros was still the emperor, much of the country had risen up against him. He was eventually driven to seek refuge in his mountain fortress in the town of Magdala. Here, he finally irked the wrath of the British. In his obsession with forcing Christian missionaries to produce arms, he confined several British subjects in Magdala against their will.

In 1862, he urged Captain Cameron, the British consul, to head to the port of Massawa, which the British frequented, to see if he might receive word from the British government. But when Cameron chose to return by way of Metemma (also sometimes called Matamma), a port then under Egyptian control, the paranoid Tewodros suspected treason and had Cameron thrown behind bars. It was fairly clear to the British that they had a madman on their hands, so they took action. The Brits entered into talks with other leading figures in Ethiopia and arranged a limited military operation with the goal of taking Tewodros into British custody and freeing the hostages.

As much as many Ethiopians today lionize Tewodros as some kind of great and heroic freedom fighter, we must consider the actual reality on the ground in Ethiopia at that time. Tewodros was not popular among most Ethiopians. Far from it. At this point in his reign, he was viewed as a ruthless, unbearable, and slightly mad dictator. Most Ethiopians wished for Tewodros to be removed from power. This is demonstrated by the fact that the British had the full cooperation of Ethiopians and local Ethiopian leaders, including the man who would ultimately replace Tewodros, Johannes IV.

The British did not have to fight their way to Tewodros's fortress in Magdala. They were helped and guided by Ethiopians who wished to see Tewodros removed from power. The British army's presence in Ethiopia was viewed as peaceful. And unlike marauding Ethiopian warlords, the British did not raid villages for food and other goods; instead, the British actually paid for them. Many local Ethiopians made a lot of money by selling their goods and services to the British army.

In the fateful year of 1868, the British arrived at the gates of Tewodros's last stronghold in Magdala, Ethiopia. The British and the emperor exchanged a few words through intermediaries in the hopes of some last-minute negotiation. But it was not to be. The British insisted that Tewodros would be treated with the greatest respect and dignity but that he must surrender and be taken into British custody, ostensibly to stand trial in Britain.

Tewodros was not about to accept this fate lying down. He refused to comply, and the British prepared their assault. The British, led by Sir Robert Napier, fielded a force of around thirty thousand and easily stormed Tewodros's compound. The few daring souls who challenged the British onslaught were quickly mowed down by British artillery. In the drama that unfolded at Magdala, the scene that has captured the most attention was the last moments of Emperor Tewodros II's life.

On April 13th, 1868, just as the British were about to storm into the very room in which Tewodros stood, he made the fateful decision to pull out his personal pistol, put it to his head, and pull the trigger. Tewodros took his own life rather than allow himself to be taken captive by the British. This final defiance has so captivated many and created the legend of Tewodros being a great freedom fighter.

Considering all of the details of the situation, such a legacy can be thoroughly debated, and one could arrive at a wide variety of views on the subject. One thing that is clear and is perhaps a bit surprising considering the terrible legacy of European colonialism is that the British kept their word. In what has occasionally perplexed some historians, once the British ensured that the mad dictator Tewodros had been neutralized and the hostages had been freed, they packed their things, thanked their Ethiopian guides, and went home. They did not overstay their welcome. They also did not interfere with or even try to influence Ethiopian affairs.

The British views on the subject were made quite clear when Queen Victoria's British Foreign Secretary Lord Stanley issued a statement. "Her Majesty's government have no concern with what might befall Abyssinia from the removal of King Theodore [Tewodros] from the country. It will in no way concern them what may be the future that awaits Abyssinia; what ruler may hold power in the country; what civil wars or commotions may arise in it. On ground of humanity Her Majesty's government would desire the country to be well governed, and the people to be contented and prosperous; but they do not consider it incumbent on them to set up or to support any form of government or any particular ruler under which it shall be carried out, in a country in which they have really no British interests to promote."

Yes, it seems that the British really did have limited objectives in Ethiopia. Just to give some perspective with events in modern times, the British approach would be similar to the United States removing Iraq's Saddam Hussein from power and then immediately leaving Iraq, never to return. History, of course, did not play out that way, and the toppling of Iraq's Saddam Hussein led to several years of US occupation. The British, on the other hand, were ready to leave as soon as Tewodros was gone and basically washed their hands of the matter afterward. "Her Majesty" wished the Ethiopians the best, but otherwise, the British had no interest in being involved in any nation-building project in

Ethiopia.

Since Ethiopia had just come out of one hundred years of infighting during the Era of the Princes, in which various regional governors constantly duked it out to become the power behind the throne, the threat of a power vacuum was really nothing new to Ethiopia. Furthermore, the various factions of Ethiopian power had already been preparing for Tewodros's removal. So, as soon as the British left, the various power brokers of Ethiopia prepared to position themselves to lead their tired and weary nation.

Chapter 5 – Emperor Johannes IV Takes the Throne

"I am not worried that the Egyptians will suddenly invade Ethiopia. Nobody who has tried that has lived to tell the story."

-Meles Zenawi

After the latest round of infighting finally came to a close, an Ethiopian nobleman by the name of Mercha Kassai was hailed as emperor. Mercha Kassai was coronated on January 12th, 1872, and given the royal appellation of Johannes IV. In truth, the faction led by Johannes IV had gained control of much of Ethiopia as far back as 1868 when the British expedition against Tewodros had taken place. This is borne out by the fact that Mercha Kassai was the most prominent figure that the British consulted with prior to crossing through territory that was largely under Kassai's control.

But even so, it took a few years after the fall of Tewodros for Johannes IV to consolidate his power and put down potential rivals so that he could officially claim the throne. As was usually the case with any claimant, efforts were made to ensure that the new emperor was, no matter how distant, from the Solomonic line. As it pertained to Mercha Kassai (Johannes IV), it was said that he was related to the granddaughter of the first emperor to take the title of Johannes—Johannes I.

Once this was all sorted out, Johannes IV set about attempting to consolidate his control over all of the far-flung regions of Ethiopia, which was by no means an easy task. But Johannes proved himself just as able diplomatically as he was militarily. Those he could not subdue by force, he coerced through diplomacy. For instance, Johannes wisely recognized the governor of Gojjam, Ras Adal Tasamma, and even gave his blessing for this powerful warlord to expand his grip farther south over the Abay River (the Blue Nile) and encroach upon the region of Shewa.

This had the effect of offsetting the ambitious governor of Shewa, who would one day become the Ethiopian emperor Menelik II. Ethiopian historian and scholar Bahru Zewde describes this as a brilliant strategy, as Johannes IV effectively played his chief rivals against each other, using Ras Adal Tasamma as the perfect counterweight to the overly ambitious Menelik II.

Along with making sure that the various governors of Ethiopia did not defect or overstep their bounds, Johannes IV, just like Tewodros before him, had to face the growing threat of Egyptian aggression. Early on in Johannes's reign, the Egyptians began to move over the Sudanese border and take up positions in Ethiopian Eritrea.

Johannes, who still maintained contact with the British due to his prior cooperation in the overthrow of Tewodros, attempted to gain British assistance. But although the British were at times sympathetic, they were as unwilling to help Johannes as they were to aid Tewodros. However, Johannes proved a much more stable and pragmatic leader. Rather than getting frustrated and overturning the whole apple cart, Johannes played it cool and developed his own unique strategies to deal with the existential threats that Ethiopia faced. Johannes was able to build up a strong army and, through various means, was able to cobble together some basic arms to supply them with.

His efforts ultimately paid off, and he secured his first major victories in 1875 and 1876 when he successfully repulsed Egyptian incursions into northern Ethiopia in what is today Eritrea. At this time, Egypt was being led by the grandson of Pasha Muhammad Ali—Ishmael Pasha. Ishmael had serious ambitions to expand

Egypt, which already controlled much of Sudan.

The first battle took place on November 16th, 1875, near the Mareb River in the northern Ethiopian town of Gundat. Here, Johannes showed himself to be a brilliant military strategist by luring the Egyptians to their deaths. Such words might sound like an exaggeration, but they are not. The invading Egyptians were overconfident, and Johannes assumed as much. He tricked the Egyptians into thinking that his army was in retreat.

Johannes pulled his troops back, and the Egyptians followed, thinking they had their enemy on the run. Right when the Egyptian forces were down in the depths of a steep valley, Johannes turned his troops around and had them blast the Egyptians to oblivion with every single firearm in their possession. According to Ethiopian scholar Bahru Zewde, this battle ended with the almost complete and utter annihilation of the Egyptian army.

Even so, this was not the end of the Egyptian menace, for Egyptian leader Ishmael doubled down and sought revenge for the loss of so many troops. He built up another force over the next few months. In the spring of 1876, he sent them to engage the Ethiopians once again near the city of Gura. Here, the Egyptians were much more cautious and generally performed better than they had in the previous engagement, but after a long bloody struggle, the Ethiopians were again victorious.

Upon defeating his foes, Johannes received the benefit of picking up Egyptian artillery, including the requisition of twenty powerful cannons. Ethiopia's victory over Egypt had some pretty serious ramifications for the Egyptians. The demoralizing defeat led to Ishmael's eventual removal from power, and it put an end to Egyptian territorial ambitions in Ethiopia. It would also inspire Sudan to shake off the yoke of Egypt as well.

As they say, hindsight is always 20/20, but it probably would have been best if Johannes had aligned with Sudan at this juncture in history. Perhaps Johannes believed that he should avoid overplaying his hand, as he sought to negotiate peace with Egypt. Diplomatic treaties were made in 1876, shortly after the Battle of Gura.

The talks would drag on over the next few years, and in the meantime, the Sudanese—likely inspired by Egypt's defeat at the hands of Ethiopia—would rise up against the Egyptians. In 1881, the Mahdist movement erupted, which combined Sudan's personal strain of Islamic radicalism with Sudanese nationalism. They vehemently rejected Egyptian occupation.

Egypt was obviously in a bad state of affairs at the time. It had been handily defeated by the Ethiopians and now had Sudan in full revolt. This would have been another perfect opportunity for Ethiopia to make an alliance with Sudan at the expense of Egypt, yet this is not what occurred. Instead, Johannes was still knee-deep in negotiations with the beleaguered Egyptians, with the British serving as mediator.

These talks resulted in the signing of the Hewett Treaty, which was overseen by British Rear Admiral Sir William Hewett. It was signed on June 3rd, 1884. The terms of this treaty initially seemed to grant much of what Johannes was looking for. Ethiopia was allowed to have "free import of goods," but most importantly, it had unrestricted access to firearms. Ill-fated former emperor Tewodros would have been ecstatic on this point alone.

The treaty also agreed to have territory previously seized by Egypt returned to Ethiopia. But as part of this bargain, Johannes had to agree to aid the evacuation of Egyptian troops from the region. These efforts brought Ethiopian troops into direct conflict with the Sudanese Mahdists who were fighting the Egyptians. Ethiopia was now in the bizarre and seemingly irrational position of having defeated the Egyptians only to have to turn around and prop them up against the Sudanese.

These developments would have direct consequences for Johannes himself since it was a battle against the resurgent Mahdists in 1889 that would lead to his death. Yes, the great Ethiopian emperor who had decisively defeated one of the greatest foes in Ethiopian history was killed in what was essentially an entirely unnecessary and senseless battle with Sudanese freedom fighters who could have been Ethiopia's allies.

The first battle against the Mahdists broke out in September 1885 when one of Johannes's loyal commanders, Ras Alula, successfully put down a few thousand Mahdist fighters, although he was injured in the melee. The Mahdists would rally, and by 1888, they reached the old capital of Ethiopia—Gondar—looting and plundering the city. Johannes IV had actually commissioned Menelik to relieve Gondor, but Menelik and his troops took too long to get there and were not of much help.

Johannes would lead a major battle against Mahdist troops situated around Metemma on March 9th, 1889. The battle initially went well for the Ethiopians, and they appeared to be on the verge of victory. However, chaos erupted when Johannes IV fell in battle. This chaos would then engulf all of Ethiopia, as Johannes IV's most likely successor—Menelik II—struggled to defeat Ethiopia's external enemies and claw his way to the throne.

Chapter 6 – Menelik II's Hard-Fought Peace

"I wanted the world to know that my country Ethiopia has always won with determination and heroism."

-Abebe Bikila

Menelik II was born in 1844, right at the height of the turbulent Era of the Princes. As a young man, he grew up under the unique but entirely unstable reign of Emperor Tewodros. Upon Tewodros's death in 1868, Menelik was a young man, still in his twenties, yet he had already created a big enough power base for himself to be a potential contender for the throne.

From the very beginning of Emperor Johannes IV's reign, Johannes had to contend with the rising power of Menelik. Initially, Johannes was quite effective at containing Menelik in the Shewa region by using other regional governors to essentially box him in and check his growth. But the two did not completely come to terms with each other until they entered into the Leche Agreement in 1878.

The agreement is called this because Johannes and Menelik had a veritable showdown near the town of Leche, where they nearly came to blows. Menelik, however, wisely realized that he was not ready to take on Johannes and ultimately yielded to the

Ethiopian emperor. Menelik officially submitted to Johannes, and Johannes gracefully accepted his submission. Johannes then dubbed Menelik as one of his faithful subordinates, making him a regional "king" as it were, and charged him to rule the region as he saw fit as long as he ultimately looked upon Emperor Johannes as his sovereign,

During this encounter, Johannes is said to have told Menelik, "You are accordingly king and master of a land conquered by your forebears; I shall respect your sovereignty if you will be faithful to the agreements decided between us. Whoever strikes your kingdom, strikes me, and whoever makes war on you, makes it on me. You are accordingly my eldest son." Ethiopia's system of regional rulers, with local warlords like Menelik being subordinate to an overarching emperor, was very much reminiscent of the feudalism of Europe during the Middle Ages. Menelik was basically the Ethiopian equivalent of an earl or baron. He was in charge of maintaining his own region as long as he ultimately reported back to Emperor Johannes at the end of the day.

A little over ten years after this agreement was reached, Emperor Johannes IV perished fighting the Sudanese Mahdists in 1889. Menelik was no doubt shocked to hear of his emperor's death, even though they had been rivals at times. But he was, nevertheless, ready for it.

Menelik had already consolidated a large army and shored up solid political connections. He even married up, wedding a noblewoman by the name of Taytu in 1883. Taytu is said to have been a direct descendant of former Emperor Susenyos I, making her of the Solomonic line. Menelik also made inroads on the international front. While Emperor Johannes was forging ties with the British with the Hewitt Treaty, which had him aiding the Egyptians against the Sudanese Mahdists, Menelik was entertaining a new international player, one who was late to the Ethiopian scene—the Italians.

Menelik had engaged in diplomatic relations with the Italians who frequented the region of Shewa in the past. However, he became deeply dismayed to learn that the British had unilaterally given the Italians access to the northern Ethiopian port of

Massawa. The Red Sea port of Massawa (part of modern-day Eritrea) was an ancient Ethiopian territory, but it had been seized several centuries prior by the Ottoman Empire. It was then in the hands of the Egyptians, and Johannes was expecting its return after Egypt's defeat.

At the last minute, the British seemingly switched the Egyptian presence for an Italian presence, hoping to use the Italians as their own personal "watchdog" on the Red Sea. This dubious and underhanded maneuver infuriated both Emperor Johannes and Menelik. In time, the Italians' entrance into Massawa would lay the groundwork for a titanic struggle between Italy and Ethiopia.

Emperor Johannes was still trying to come to grips with this situation when he was taken out by the Mahdists in 1889. Thus, Menelik would have to deal with the Italians. Even though all the Italians had been granted was a toehold in the Red Sea port, it was not long before they found any excuse they could to expand their reach farther out into the highlands of northern Ethiopia. The Italians severely overstepped their bounds by 1887, and one of Emperor Johannes's henchmen—Ras Alula—bared his teeth. His militia engaged the Italians at Dogali and soundly defeated them, leaving hundreds of Italian troops dead. In truth, the Italians were more or less ambushed, and back in Italy, the incident was referred to as a massacre. It was not long before both the Italian Parliament and the average Italian on the street were calling for vengeance.

Italy's efforts of expansion would continue. Soon, Italian forces would be expanding into the nearby settlement of Saati. The Italians were quite busy here, laying down railroad tracks and even a telegraph line. To prevent any future ambushes, the settlement was surrounded by floodlights, which were run off a generator. The Italians even floated a man up in a hot air balloon just so he could keep watch. The Italians were indeed ready to use the latest in technology to improve their odds.

By the time Menelik came to the throne, he was not ready for war. So, he attempted to use diplomacy by utilizing an old resource: Italian diplomat Count Pietro Antonelli. As a result, Menelik forged the Treaty of Wuchale with the Italians. Menelik gave up much of what is today Eritrea, among other things, but the biggest issue was over Ethiopian sovereignty. The treaty had a stipulation that Ethiopia must defer to Italy when it came to important international situations. Such a pledge would take away Ethiopia's freedom as an independent nation and essentially reduce Ethiopia to being a protectorate of Italy.

Menelik was tricked into signing off on this agreement due to some sleight of hand by the Italians. Even though the agreement to a protectorate status was included in the Italian copy of the agreement, in the Amharic version, it most certainly was not. This can hardly be viewed as an accident on the Italians' part.

At any rate, Menelik had no idea what he was being forced to agree to by signing his name. When the Italian version was properly translated to Menelik, he was deeply dismayed but managed to keep his composure. Apparently hoping that the whole "misunderstanding" could be cleared up diplomatically, he fired off a missive to Rome in an effort to set the record straight. The letter heavily referenced the aforementioned Italian diplomat Antonelli, indicating just how involved this Italian technocrat was with Ethiopian affairs at the time.

The letter read in part, "I was astounded when I saw what Antonelli brought me. Even in our country when merchants ask a price, they ask for more than its value so they can go down to its true value; they do not set a low price so as to increase it after. When Antonelli demanded the frontier at the Mereb, I told him, 'If I am called King of Kings of Ethiopia it is because I have Tigray in my kingdom. If you take up to the Mereb, what is left for me?' The hereditary lords of Tigray protested me, 'How can you let Italy take that country which we kept at the price of our blood fighting the [Egyptians]?' I told them it was better to have Christians as neighbors than Muslims and that peace was better than war. I ordered Dejasmach Meshesha Werqe to make peace between Ras Mengesha, Ras Alula and your generals. They made peace. Then I gave all honors to your envoy Count Salimbeni and asked him, 'Why is the border delineation not done?' He told me it cannot be done until you possess the Mereb as frontier. I know such words could not come from your mouth as Ras Makonnen spoke highly of your royal character. I am waiting impatiently for this frontier to be settled."

This letter from Menelik, while ostensibly still seeking a diplomatic solution, was unabashedly angry, as indicated by the words "I am waiting impatiently for this frontier to be settled." Upon reading it, one could almost wonder if that was a typo, but unless it was a Freudian slip on Menelik's part, he likely used this word with his translators on purpose to convey to the Italians that his patience with them had just about run out.

The situation between the Italians and the Ethiopians during this period is more complicated than many accounts seem to acknowledge. The short, oversimplified version of events says the Italians were evil, horrible colonizers who wrongly inserted themselves into Ethiopian affairs and that the Ethiopians ultimately prevailed and shook off their oppressors. But it really is much more complex than such a simple summarization of events.

The Italians had been on friendly terms with the Ethiopians since the days of Emperor Johannes and had made significant inroads with his successor Menelik prior to him coming to the throne. It is for this reason that Menelik's court was swimming with Italian diplomats when the "misunderstanding" over the Treaty of Wuchale took place.

The first hint of a problem occurred when the British, in the aftermath of the Egyptian defeat, betrayed Ethiopian interests by unilaterally ceding the port of Massawa to the Italians. This gave the Italians a colonial foothold in northern Ethiopia. The Italians then pressed their luck and attempted to encroach farther into the Ethiopian highlands. Their actions provoked a major Ethiopian response.

The fact that Ethiopian troops under Ras Alula decimated hundreds of Italians in one battle was no small thing. In many ways, it is amazing that total war did not erupt right then and there. But it did not. It seems that, for various reasons, both the Italians and Ethiopians wanted to dial back the temperature and give peace (or at least some variation of it) a chance.

At this point, the Italians were poking and prodding, attempting to ascertain how best to approach the Ethiopians. They clearly wanted to gain concessions from Ethiopia, but they were not yet willing to go to war to do it. Instead, they attempted to dupe Menelik through diplomatic duplicity. When Menelik understood the games that the Italians were playing, he decided to drop the pretenses and call them out on it.

In his angry letter, Menelik even mentioned the massacre at Dogali and spoke of how he had since ordered his commanders to cease their hostilities and made great efforts to maintain peace. This offhand reference to the Dogali incident was likely a way to show himself as a peacemaker while subtly threatening the Italians with a reminder of how they were dealt a decisive blow by the Ethiopians.

The Italians could have backed down at this point. They could have even sought to save face by claiming the situation truly was just a big misunderstanding. But they did not. Rather than learning their lesson after their troops were destroyed at Dogali, they listened to the loud, angry voices in both the Italian Parliament and the Italian streets. The people called for aggressive action against Ethiopia. Italy, no matter how arrogant and self-righteous it was, felt as if it could not back down.

Italy had only become a unified nation a few decades prior, in 1871, so it was quite anxious to prove itself while all of its European peers were watching. Italy's anxiety of being made to "look bad" in front of other European powers was openly expressed to Menelik at the time by his resident Italian diplomat Antonelli, who warned him of the dangers of "embarrassing" Italy before other European nations.

Nevertheless, Menelik sent out a series of correspondence to just about all of the major players in the world at the time, indicating that Ethiopia had been duped by the Italians and that the treaty was, therefore, null and void. But rather than admit their fault, the self-conscious Italians doubled down. They insisted they were not to blame for this diplomatic debacle and that it was the Ethiopians who were mistaken.

Count Antonelli worked hard to ease tensions as much as possible. His needling initially paid off. In early 1891, he seemed to be on the verge of a breakthrough compromise with Menelik.

Menelik agreed to an adjustment of the Italian terms in which he would consider giving Italy a preferred status, not protectorate status. He also pledged not to allow any other nation to claim a protectorate over Ethiopia. Since Menelik had no intention of allowing Ethiopia to become a protectorate of any nation, this was obviously agreeable. By declaring that Ethiopia would not allow any other nation to claim it as a protectorate, the Italians would save some face since it rendered them the preferred candidate should Ethiopia ever change its mind.

It all seems fairly absurd, but Antonelli was attempting to wrangle a diplomatic miracle to avert war by vigorously massaging the fine print of the treaty. Although Menelik initially seemed agreeable to these possible modifications, his wife, Empress Taytu, was aghast. It is said that she often interrupted the proceedings to voice her concerns.

At one point, Antonelli again explained the importance of Italy not being embarrassed on the world stage. Taytu had something to say. According to accounts of the exchange, Taytu angrily remarked, "We too must maintain our dignity! You want other countries to see Ethiopia as your protégé, but that will never be!" Yes, as strong of a leader as Menelik was, there are many accounts taken directly from Ethiopian court proceedings that indicate his wife had quite a bit of influence when it came to diplomatic relations. This was something that Italian diplomats, such as Antonelli, often complained about. They seemed to view Emperor Menelik as the more malleable partner of the royal pair and the empress as more of a foil to their schemes.

Empress Taytu ultimately got the last laugh with Antonelli when, in February of 1891, he was beaten at his own game. After heated deliberation, he was tricked into signing a new treaty written in Amharic, which Antonelli thought would confirm Italy's preferred status. Shortly after signing it, he translated the document to find that it was a complete rejection of any and all possibility of Ethiopia becoming a protectorate.

Realizing he had just been tricked into signing his own name on the polar opposite of what the Italian government wanted, Antonelli lost his diplomatic cool and ripped his signed name off the document. Later accounts say that Empress Taytu was quite amused by the incident, but she also rebuked Antonelli for being so brash and rightfully pointed out that no one had forced him to sign the treaty.

Shortly after this incident, Antonelli and other Italian diplomats departed from Ethiopia. Emperor Menelik II was happy to have stood his ground, but he must have known that the departure of these diplomats symbolized the departure of any chance of success as it pertained to diplomacy. There were some meager attempts, such as in the summer of 1894 when a new diplomatic mission briefly appeared at Emperor Menelik's court in Addis Ababa, but the efforts went nowhere. War with Italy was indeed on the horizon.

Interestingly enough, as both sides marched ever closer to blows, a Russian delegation arrived in Ethiopia. The delegation arrived in early 1895 and presented itself as a goodwill mission with a heavy interest in shoring up religious and political relations between Ethiopia and Russia. Ethiopia and Russia did have something in common because they were both Orthodox Christians.

Menelik was pleased to be able to meet up with supposed co-religionists and also did not fail to see the opportunity of gaining military support from another European power. This first Russian mission to Ethiopia resulted in an immediate return mission, as Ethiopian diplomats arrived in Russia in June 1895. The Italians were deeply suspicious and worried about these developments, but the Russians insisted that no formal military alliance was being made.

Nevertheless, the Ethiopian delegation was quietly gifted with some 135 Russian-made artillery pieces to take home with them. After a whirlwind affair in Russia, the Ethiopian entourage returned to Ethiopia through the port of Djibouti on September 2nd, 1895. Russian aid may have been minimal, but even the idea that another European power was interested in supporting Ethiopia against the Italians was a great morale booster for Emperor Menelik. Italy, too, must have sensed that with Russia weighing in, international opinion might soon turn against them.

As such, Italy decided to act.

Italy made its first outwardly aggressive move in October 1895 by crossing over the Mareb River, which had previously represented a border for territorial expansion. Menelik's response was quick and decisive. He cobbled together a huge army of 100,000 troops, which were armed as best as Menelik could manage.

With his army ready to march, a carefully prepared statement was issued from Menelik that read in part, "Assemble the army, beat the drum. God, in his bounty, has struck down my enemies and enlarged my empire and preserved me to this day. I have reigned by the grace of God. As we must all die—I will not be afflicted if I die. Enemies have come who would ruin our country and change our religion [from Orthodox to Catholicism]. They have passed beyond the sea that God gave us for our frontier. I, aware that herds were decimated and people were exhausted, did not wish to do anything [about it] until now. These enemies have advanced, burrowing into the country like moles. With God's help, I will get rid of them. Men of my country, up to now, I believe I have never wronged you, and you have never caused pain to me. Now—you who are strong help me—you who are weak help with your prayers, while you think of your children, your wife and your faith."

It was a powerful unifying statement to bring together Ethiopians while dehumanizing the enemy Italians as nothing more than moles—intrusive pests—that needed to be done away with. With these popular sentiments proclaimed, the Ethiopian army was sent to meet the Italian threat head-on. This led to the first real engagement, which occurred in the vicinity of Amba Alagi in the Ethiopian region of Tigray on December 7th, 1895.

A contingent of Ethiopian troops under the leadership of Fitawrari Gebeyehu approached a fortified Italian compound. A skirmish broke out between this advance guard of Ethiopians and the Italians. Soon, the rest of the Ethiopian troops rushed forward to reinforce Gebeyehu's contingent. The Italian fortress was situated on top of a hill, which meant the Ethiopians had to struggle their way up an incline just to reach the fortification.

It certainly was an uphill battle, but nevertheless, the Ethiopians overwhelmed their enemy and defeated them, seizing the fortress. It has been said that over one thousand Italian troops perished in this exchange. Fitawrari Gebeyehu was hailed as a hero and given the nickname of "Gobez-ayehu." It is a play on words with the name "Gebeyehu." In Amharic, the word "gobez" means "good," but affixed to "ayehu," it means something along the lines of "good, brave man."

After this successful assault, the Ethiopian army moved on to a nearby Italian fort, located in Tigray's Mekelle, where some of the previous Italian combatants had fled. Surrounded and out of supplies, the Italians surrendered. The Ethiopians generously allowed them to leave the fort and even supplied them with much-needed water and other provisions.

At this point, Emperor Menelik had not completely given up on peace and was perhaps hoping this display of mercy would convince the Italians to come back to the negotiating table. But the Italian government back in Rome remained entirely insolent and stubborn and refused to budge on any of its previous positions. Thus, the war carried on.

Shortly after Mekelle was seized, the final dramatic encounter of the war occurred. Menelik marched his troops toward the Italian stronghold of Adwa in the spring of 1896. Menelik's army was camped outside of Adwa's gates in the early hours of March 1st. The Italian commander, Oreste Baratieri, rolled the dice and decided to send his troops outside the protection of the fortress to attempt an offensive against the Ethiopians.

A depiction of Menelik II at the Battle of Adwa.

Baratieri led three columns of troops toward the Ethiopian army. From the beginning of the battle, logistics and coordination proved to be severely lacking on the Italians' part. And soon, a ferocious Ethiopian response began tearing into Italian lines. Chaos ensued. The Italian troops were decimated, and once the smoke cleared on that fateful day of March 1st, 1896, it was clear that Italy had lost the war. The Italian troops were almost utterly annihilated, and those who survived had to deal with the harsh reality of being a prisoner of war.

Most of the Italians were generally cared for, but a few came out the worse for wear due to some of Menelik's more overzealous troops. Quite frankly, the worst fate an Italian soldier could expect was being castrated. As horrible as it sounds (and it most certainly is terrible), for some Ethiopian soldiers, the taking of their enemy's testicles was considered a trophy of war. For the record, Menelik is said to have forbidden the exercise and expressly denounced those who did it. But then, as is the case now, even the best military commanders cannot fully control the actions of all of their soldiers. So yes, abuses did occur, but it should not reflect upon the Ethiopian troops as a whole but rather just the most extreme among them.

At any rate, the humiliated and defeated Italians had no choice but to negotiate with Ethiopia. This led to the signing of the Treaty of Addis Ababa in October 1896. Italy finally recognized the complete and unalterable independence of Ethiopia. The formal recognition of Ethiopia as an independent power on the world stage was considered a great prize for Ethiopian prestige. Overall, though, the treaty was fairly lenient on the Italians. The Ethiopians did not make any new territorial demands. The Italians were forced to go back to the territory they had controlled in the northernmost reaches of Ethiopia (modern-day Eritrea) prior to the conflict.

However, this would come back to haunt Ethiopia in later decades when fascist Italian dictator Benito Mussolini used Italian Eritrea as a launching pad for further hostilities against Ethiopia. For a time, though, it seemed that Menelik had won a hard-fought peace, and all of Ethiopia was proud of what had been achieved.

Chapter 7 – Menelik II's Later Years and the Arrival of Ras Tafari

"You must always remember that to lead, one must first learn to follow."

-Haile Selassie

Menelik II's victory over the Italians shocked the world and gained Ethiopia hard-won prestige. But there were still troubling realities on the ground Ethiopia had to deal with. Just prior to the war, famine had rocked the country and left many dead, and in the years immediately following the conflict, Menelik had to deal with rebellious governors in various regions of his empire.

A photograph of Menelik II.

For instance, the governor of Tigray, where much of the fighting against encroaching Italians took place, began to rattle his saber against Menelik. This rebellion was put down by Menelik in 1902, but shortly after, Menelik had to put out another fire when the Oromo people of southern Ethiopia began to rebel against his rule.

Menelik also faced trouble from perhaps an unsuspected quarter due to the ambitious pretenses of the governor of Harar in eastern Ethiopia—Ras Makonnen. Ras Makonnen had shown valor and distinction when leading troops in the fight against the Italians, and he now seemed poised to position himself as the ultimate heir to the throne. This was, after all, the general tradition of succession in Ethiopia ever since the Era of the Princes. Usually, the emperor's hereditary children did not succeed the throne; more often than not, a regional "prince" or governor would take control.

Menelik likely viewed Ras Makonnen as a worthy successor since he described their relationship as being akin to "father and son." But Menelik hoped to have longevity on his side and did not want his "son" to get any funny ideas and attempt to succeed him too soon. As fate would have it, Ras Makonnen would not ultimately succeed Menelik. After a long struggle, his son, Tafari Makonnen, later Ras Tafari, would receive that honor.

At any rate, despite some regional instability, Menelik began to make progress on the domestic front. With the aid of French engineers, he had a railroad installed that reached from Djibouti in the north all the way to Addis Ababa, the capital, located in the center of Ethiopia. This rail line would be a boon to both Ethiopia and foreign travelers since it meant that the dangerous overland trek from the port of Djibouti to Addis Ababa would no longer be necessary.

In previous years, Ras Makonnen's domain of Harar had received a great way to interconnect with the rest of Ethiopia due to the installation of a working telegraph. It connected the easternmost reaches of Ethiopia to the capital city. The telegraph was soon updated to telephones. Addis Ababa was hooked up to telephones in Tigray and Eritrea by 1904 and to Gore by 1905.

The railroad, telegraph, and telephone proved to be great assets for Menelik's empire since they allowed him to have much easier contact with the representatives of various regions. This aided in creating a better sense of centralization; previously, the government had been a loosely connected federation.

In the following year, 1906, Menelik began considering who his heir might be. The first in line was Zewditu (also sometimes spelled as Zawditu), his daughter, followed by his grandson, a young man by the name of Lij Iyasu. But Menelik changed his mind, as he felt that Ras Makonnen would be the most reliable choice.

Ras Makonnen, the governor of Harar, had already proved himself to be a formidable military commander and civil administrator. Yet, sadly enough, right when Menelik II was about to make his decision known, Ras Makonnen abruptly passed away. As sad as the passing was for Menelik, it was absolutely devastating for his son, Tafari. The most immediate effect it had on him was that the fourteen-year-old was expected to take his place as the Ras of Harar. This would give him the title that Jamaicans would later make famous, Ras Tafari, since young Tafari would be the Ras (governor) of Harar.

But Menelik felt the youngster was not quite ready and had Ras Tafari come to Addis Ababa so that he could be more adequately trained in government. Tafari's half-brother, Yilma, would govern Harar while Tafari was away. Interestingly, Menelik's grandson, who was also a potential successor, attended the same school in which Tafari was enrolled.

Emperor Menelik suffered a stroke on October 27th, 1909, and from this point forward, his health took a sharp downturn. But whereas the young Tafari seemed to take his training quite seriously, Lij Iyasu was known more for blowing his grandfather's money and hanging out with his friends.

Tafari would receive word in 1907 that his half-brother Yilma had died. This meant that it was incumbent upon Tafari to become the Ras of Harar. However, before he could claim the title of Ras Tafari, Menelik intervened by placing one of his military commanders, a man by the name of Balcha Safo, in the position. And instead of sending Tafari to Harar, Menelik had him posted as an administrator in the region of Sidamo.

Tafari promptly arrived in Sidamo accompanied by his own militia, which had been loyal to his father, the deceased Ras Makonnen. Tafari quickly got to business in Sidamo and sought to familiarize himself with the people under his jurisdiction. He held weekly councils with his associates to discuss all of the pertinent matters of the day. Tafari was quite content in his new role but still kept an eye on the future.

In 1909, Tafari cast his eyes back to the capital after learning that Menelik had suffered a massive stroke. This stroke was more dire than the last, and it was clear to all that Menelik, even if he were to live a few more years, would not be the same again. Movement and even the ability to speak became a challenge for him.

Tafari knew that he was a candidate for the throne, so he immediately returned to Addis Ababa to see what fate might have in store for him. Since Menelik had become largely incapacitated, Empress Taytu was ruling in his stead. It would soon become known that Menelik had chosen his grandson, Lij Iyasu, to replace him. Even though this was one of her ailing husband's last wishes, the strong-willed Taytu almost immediately went against them.

Both she and Menelik's daughter from a previous marriage, Princess Zewditu, began to conspire against the decision. As much as Menelik might have loved his grandson, they just did not see the freewheeling Iyasu as a good candidate to lead Ethiopia. Due to this conniving and other political differences, various factions began to rise up against Empress Taytu. Suddenly surrounded by a hostile camp of ministers, Taytu was forced to go into retirement in the spring of 1910.

Tafari attempted to pretend not to be interested in taking a side. His neutrality was rewarded by being given back his predestined role of Ras of Harar. At this point, the young Ras Tafari exited the picture and went back to Harar while the imperial court in Addis Ababa continued to duke it out.

As it pertains to Harar, its denizens were quite happy to have their favored son return. Ras Tafari's father, Ras Makonnen, was very popular among the Harar people. He was known as a strong but fair leader who treated all of the residents of the region with respect. Ras Tafari's half-brother, who had temporarily filled in for him after their father's passing, was seen as an abusive tyrant who overly taxed the people to the point of poverty. Tafari's return was seen as a breath of fresh air. And for the most part, Ras Tafari lived up to his father's name, proving himself an able and fair governor of Harar.

Ras Tafari was indeed a wise ruler. In 1911, he further showed his pragmatism by making the fateful decision to marry Princess Menen Asfaw, who was actually Iyasu's niece. The future successor of Menelik was still far from certain at this time, but Ras Tafari knew the value of political marriages. He sought to draw his fortunes closer to the center of power in Addis Ababa. Even though his marriage was, in many ways, one of convenience, it has been said that Ras Tafari loved his wife. During their long marriage, he would have six children with her.

Emperor Menelik II finally succumbed to his poor health, passing away on December 12th, 1913. This made Lij Iyasu the de facto ruler of Ethiopia, even though he had not been officially crowned. Almost immediately, there was pushback against Iyasu. The old faction that had been led by Empress Taytu soon reemerged and began plotting to avert the crowning of the would-be emperor.

A photograph of Lij Iyasu.

https://en.wikipedia.org/wiki/File:Yasu_V.jpg

Iyasu was not seen as a serious candidate, and there were also rumblings that Iyasu was an adherent to Islam. Ethiopia was a Christian kingdom; its Christian background stretched back nearly two thousand years. Thus, such things were not looked on too favorably. He also appointed a Muslim to his cabinet, which was frowned upon. Considering the mindset of Ethiopians back then, it is no wonder that Iyasu's decision to appoint an openly practicing Muslim, a man named Hasib Ydlibi from Harar, as one of his top ministers of government caused a stir in Ethiopia.

Ethiopia had been fighting wars against external threats from neighboring Islamic nations for centuries and had a deep-seated fear of Islam somehow taking root and taking over from within. However irrational this might sound, many feared that Islamic administrators were being placed in the highest posts in government. The news of Ydlibi's appointment deeply alarmed Ras Tafari, who was immediately affected since much of his efforts to improve taxation in Harar were sidelined by sudden reforms coming from the top.

Ras Tafari had more changes in store. In 1916, Iyasu ordered him to relocate from Harar; he was sent to serve as the Ras of Kaffa. Being completely uprooted like this was very upsetting to Ras Tafari. He and his family had deep roots in Harar, and he had no desire to be relocated. It was at this point that Tafari decided to actively work to undermine Iyasu. He was not yet ready to oppose him outright, but he began to quietly work behind the scenes, pulling other fellow malcontents over to his side as they held their breath and waited for an opportunity to strike.

Iyasu caused even more worry during the outbreak of World War One, as he wished to side with the Central Powers. The Central Powers were Germany, Austria-Hungary, and the Ottoman Empire, and they were pitted against the Allies, which consisted of Britain, France, Russia, and later the United States. The most galling aspect of all of this for the Ethiopians was the idea that Ethiopia would support the Ottoman Turks, whom most still viewed as their ancestral enemy.

It is not entirely clear how committed young Iyasu was in his support, but the Allies picked up on the chatter and took it seriously enough to place an arms embargo on Ethiopia. The Allies then drafted an official letter of protest on September 12th, 1916, and sent it directly to Ethiopia's Foreign Ministry, demanding to know what Iyasu's intentions were.

Iyasu was not only causing trouble at home but was also stirring up problems abroad with potentially catastrophic consequences. The situation had become intolerable for Iyasu's opposition, and they decided that it was time to act. One by one, almost all of the nobility turned against Iyasu. In a conference held on September 27th, 1916, charges of "apostasy" were leveled at Iyasu. (Apostasy is a bit of an outdated term nowadays, but back in the day, the term was used to describe one who had walked away from their faith. Here, Iyasu was being accused of walking away from the traditional Ethiopian religion of Christianity in favor of Islam.)

Due to the charges leveled against him, Iyasu completely lost any real control over his subordinates and was promptly excommunicated from the Ethiopian Orthodox Church and forced to give up any claim to the Ethiopian crown. Iyasu's brief reign was over. Ethiopian ministers then turned toward Menelik's daughter, Zewditu, and decided to make her empress.

However, they understood this move would be another interlude until a longer-lasting candidate for emperor could be put in place. After some discussion, it was determined that Ras Tafari, the son of Menelik's trusted friend Ras Makonnen, would be the best choice. Iyasu was away from the capital when all of this took place, but as soon as he learned of it, he headed back to Addis Ababa.

He was far too late to stop what had already been set in motion. By the time he and his entourage reached the halfway point, between the cities of Dire Dawa and Addis Ababa, they were intercepted by some fifteen thousand troops that were ready to take the former heir apparent of Ethiopia into custody. Iyasu knew he could not win by force, so he turned and took off for the remote region of Afar. He would hide out from his enemies for the next few years until he was ultimately captured in 1921.

His father, Mikael Ali, who governed Wollo and had a substantial standing militia of his own, was not going to take the deposition of his son lying down. He raised up around eighty thousand loyal troops. On October 17th, 1916, he sent them marching on Addis Ababa in a bid to take back the throne for his son by force. This armed contingent only made it within 80 miles of the capital before they were confronted by a host of federal troops from the central government some 120,000 strong. Judging by the numbers, the latter should have trounced the former. But that is not what happened.

For whatever reason, Mikael's soldiers seemed to fight harder, and after a bloody struggle, they managed to gain the upper hand. Knowing the battle had been lost, Minister of War Fitawari Habte Giyorgis Dinagde decided the best thing he could do was buy time until reinforcements could arrive. He did so by feigning submission to Mikael. According to Ethiopian scholar Bahru Zewde, he sent out several "conciliatory messages," which made Mikael believe that the war was already won.

Mikael was ready to consolidate his gains when, days later, an even larger force from the government rammed right into his encampment. This group managed to encircle the whole of Mikael's army and deal them a decisive defeat in which Mikael was taken prisoner. With Mikael's defeat, any real hope of fugitive Prince Iyasu retaking the throne was over.

Zewditu was coronated as empress on February 11th, 1917. From the beginning, it was clear that the designated heir, Ras Tafari, would be the one making the vital decisions, while Empress Zewditu largely served as a symbolic head of state. Although he was not called as such, Ras Tafari, in many ways, acted as a prime minister, handling the most pressing matters of state. Empress Zewditu was mainly stuck with non-policy binding formalities, such as entertaining other foreign heads of state and attending special ceremonies.

Having said that, whatever direction Tafari wished to steer Ethiopian policy in, he had to have Empress Zewditu's approval first. So even though she was not as involved in policy-making, it was entirely her prerogative as to whether she signed off on proposed policies or not.

One of the most important policy decisions Tafari made early on was to seek entry into the League of Nations. Established in 1919 on the heels of World War One, the League of Nations was an international body and precursor of what would become the

United Nations. Showing how farsighted he could be, Tafari realized that Ethiopia needed more international support and felt that being part of such a prominent international body would be highly beneficial for Ethiopia.

However, Tafari met severe headwinds in trying to do so. First and foremost, the League of Nations rejected Ethiopia's application because Ethiopia had never fully abolished slavery. Yes, while much of the rest of the world had long ago jettisoned the horrid notion that one could enslave another human being, in certain regions of Ethiopia, there were instances of slavery taking place. The more affluent Ethiopians would have lifelong "servants" (in other words, slaves) under their direct control. The institution had been so ingrained in Ethiopian culture that it was difficult to remove the practice entirely.

The Ethiopian government's failure to completely abolish slavery was the main reason for Ethiopia being denied a seat in the League of Nations. International condemnation led Tafari to take measures to begin the process of abolition. In 1918, he issued a proclamation that the actual trade of slaves would be banned. This did not end the practice entirely, but it prevented any further trading of slaves.

Tafari was fully aware of the daunting task he faced in rooting out a practice that had become so ingrained in Ethiopian society, and he attempted to explain his difficult position to the international community. He pledged to those concerned that he was doing everything he could to educate his countrymen about the need to end slavery but that it would take some time to complete the process.

After much petitioning and pledges to address human rights, Ethiopia was finally granted admission into the League of Nations in 1923. Tafari hoped that the collective security of the League of Nations would protect Ethiopia against foreign threats so that he could focus on the more pressing problems at home. These were indeed Tafari's two main objectives: securing peace abroad and stability at home. And for Tafari, home primarily meant Addis Ababa, the capital city, where most of his reforms became visible.

Around this time, Tafari was instrumental in establishing things like Ethiopia's own printing press and, in 1923, its own newspaper, Berhanena Selam, which catered to a fairly new class of Ethiopians—city dwellers. Tafari knew how important education was and established many modern schools to train the new generation of Ethiopians. In 1925, he commissioned the Tafari Makonnen School, which became a major focal point of learning for those who wished to enter Ethiopia's budding civil service.

The previous year, Tafari had gone on a long overseas tour to promote awareness of Ethiopia's growing stature and to gain insight from foreign peers on various modes of reform. One of the trip's highlights occurred on April 14th, 1924, when Tafari and his entourage visited the Holy Land and made a pilgrimage to Jerusalem.

Tafari was quite religious, so it is no surprise he wanted to visit the sacred sites of Jerusalem. But there was also a lot of valuable symbolism involved for him as the heir apparent. Jerusalem was a city that many other great Ethiopian emperors had either visited or made proposals to visit. Ethiopian Emperor Lalibela, for example, was so inspired by Jerusalem that he attempted to build his own version of it in northern Ethiopia. The fact that Tafari was able to go to Jerusalem in person was a point of pride and great esteem. While he was there, he was able to secure permission for the Ethiopian clergy to make use of the Greek Orthodox monastery located on Mount Golgotha, which was certainly welcome and happy news for the Ethiopian Orthodox Church.

Tafari and company arrived in Paris, France, on May 15th. He was eager to talk with French officials about the possibility of Ethiopia gaining access to the sea through one of the French-controlled Red Sea ports. However, the French made it clear that they were not interested, so the talks quickly went nowhere.

One of the most interesting stops Tafari and his entourage made was in the homeland of Ethiopia's old nemesis, Italy. By the 1920s, both Ethiopia and Italy had tried to mend fences and held superficial respect for each other. In truth, the Italians, despite their previous trespasses, made a good show of affection to the Ethiopian delegation when they appeared in Rome that June.

Tafari and his associates were treated to lavish banquets in their honor, and the new Italian prime minister, Benito Mussolini, was all smiles and warm handshakes for his guests.

Such things are hard to fathom, considering the fact that ten years later, Mussolini would lead an Italian invasion of Ethiopia. But back in 1924, the Italians—at least on the surface—seemed as friendly as could be. The atmosphere seemed right for Tafari to talk to the Italians about his quest for a port to the Red Sea. Since the Italians controlled Eritrea, which was north of Ethiopia, it was hoped that some sort of compromise could be made to gain access.

Mussolini did have a suggestion. He immediately turned Tafari's attention to the port of Assab in Eritrea. Mussolini then hammered out a deal that would essentially allow Ethiopia to control the port for a total of ninety-nine years as long as Italy was given favored trading status with Ethiopia. As Tafari and company were considering all of the finer details of being locked into a long-term agreement with Italy, memories of the former dubiousness of Italian agreements likely came to mind. Ultimately, Tafari was moved to forego the proposed arrangement.

Upon Tafari's return to Ethiopia that September, he had learned much but was a bit disappointed that he did not have any solid policy gains from his time abroad. However, shortly thereafter, in March of 1925, he would receive a great morale booster when the French, along with some other members of the League of Nations, agreed to drop the arms embargo that had been placed on Ethiopia. This allowed Ethiopia to build up its depleted armed forces.

Hundreds of machine guns and other artillery began to flow in from countries like Switzerland and even Czechoslovakia. Tafari was always aware of Ethiopia's need to have modern arms to defend itself and was greatly encouraged by this result.

Ethiopia's membership in the League of Nations would bear fruit when Italy attempted to violate Ethiopian integrity by running a rail line from Italian Somaliland to Italian Eritrea, which went through part of Ethiopia. Italy did not seek permission to do this. Yes, as friendly as Mussolini and his cronies had acted, Ethiopia was given a reminder of how duplicitous Italy could be. Upon learning that such plans were underway, Tafari went directly to the League of Nations to demand an explanation for this blatant violation. After doing so, the plans were immediately nixed, and Ethiopia's sovereignty was respected. If Ethiopia had not been a member of the League of Nations, it would not have had powerful enough diplomatic channels to enforce international norms.

For Tafari, this was a great victory, as he did not have to fire a single bullet. For the most part, Tafari's early administration was fairly peaceful and harmonious, but a severe disturbance would erupt in 1928 when the Ethiopian region of Sidamo rose up in revolt. To this day, Sidamo is well known for the excellent coffee that is grown there. Back then, as is the case now, coffee was a major cash crop in the region. The contention began when Tafari discovered that the local administrator, Balcha Safo, was not supplying honest figures in regards to the proceeds that were being made.

So, quite naturally, like any centralized authority figure would do when a local administrator is found in error, Tafari requested Balcha Safo to come to the capital to explain himself. Safo obeyed the order, but he showed up in Addis Ababa with a large militia. The troops of this Sidamo coffee king remained on the edge of town while Safo made his way to the imperial palace.

If his intimidating escort was not enough of a forewarning, as soon as Safo began speaking with Tafari, Safo made it clear that he had no intention of taking any further orders from him. Nevertheless, Tafari stood firm, and after Safo roundly rejected his authority, he rejected Safo, informing him that he would be removed from his post. Safo then rode off to reunite with the armed encampment he had left behind, fully intending to march on the capital. But he was in for a surprise.

Demonstrating both incredible foresight and a nimble ability to orchestrate multiple events at once, Tafari had already taken measures to counteract Safo. While Safo was speaking with him, Tafari sent his troops out to threaten, bribe, or otherwise disperse Safo's militia. Safo was dismissed, and his means of reprisal were dismissed as well.

On the heels of this domestic victory, Tafari was officially declared "negus" or "king" by Empress Zewditu on September 22nd, 1928. To be clear, he was not yet emperor or the "king of kings," but he was essentially just one step away from the ultimate prize.

However, Tafari soon gained an enemy in the form of a powerful regional governor named Ras Gugsa Wolie, who just so happened to be Zewditu's husband. Yes, Ethiopian dynastic politics was indeed complicated, and although Zewditu had been pressured into crowning Tafari as king, her own husband was so resentful of the supposed diminishing of his wife's power that he rose up in revolt.

By 1929, Gugsa Wolie, despite being the empress's estranged husband, was declared an outlaw. Gugsa and Zewditu were apparently never really all that close. They practically lived separate lives. Even so, he was heavily invested in the notion of Zewditu retaining her power. If anything else, her remaining on the throne ensured his own vested interests and privileges.

Nevertheless, Tafari sent in the troops in February 1929. Upon reaching Gugsa's regional stronghold, the mere sight of Tafari's troops caused many of Gugsa's soldiers to defect. His call to arms would lead to the Battle of Anchem, which took place on March 31st, 1930.

It must be said that this engagement really was not as much a battle as it was a massacre. For the first time in history, the Ethiopian army utilized airplanes and dropped incendiaries on Gugsa's militia. The soldiers on the ground understandably panicked and began running off in all directions. In what must have seemed both absurd and dramatic, Gugsa was suddenly seen in the center of the field on top of his white stallion, all alone as his troops fled.

Gugsa was basically turned into target practice as approaching government troops used their machine guns to riddle him with bullets. This horrific spectacle was not too dissimilar from the atrocities the Italians would later commit against the Ethiopian armed forces.

Sadly enough, the very next day, on April 1st, 1930, Empress Zewditu perished from a bout of paratyphoid fever. It has been said that she was bedridden when the Battle of Anchem took place, and it remains unclear if she ever learned what happened to her estranged husband.

Yet, like clockwork, time marches inexorably on. A very rapid series of events took place. On March 31st, Ras Gugsa was killed. On April 1st, Empress Zewditu died. And then, on April 2nd, Tafari was finally crowned emperor, taking the imperial title of Haile Selassie.

A photograph of Haile Selassie.

https://en.wikipedia.org/wiki/File:Haile_Selassie_in_full_dress_(cropped).jpg

Chapter 8 – Ethiopia's Last Emperor: Haile Selassie

"Do not worship me, I am not God. I'm only a man. I worship Jesus Christ."

-Haile Selassie

Haile Selassie did not waste time consolidating his imperial power once he became emperor. He had a new national constitution for Ethiopia drawn up in 1931, which enshrined his absolute authority to make ministerial appointments, exact justice, appropriate land, and declare war. The latter of which would soon come into play. On December 5th, 1934, an incident between Ethiopian and Italian soldiers sparked a conflict.

On this date, near Italian Somaliland, a group of Ethiopians and Italians engaged in a border skirmish. The Ethiopians got the worst of it. But even so, the Italian government sought any reason to make demands of Ethiopia and held the Ethiopians entirely responsible. The Italians immediately insisted on reparations for the loss of life. Selassie, as he was accustomed to doing, immediately took the dispute to the League of Nations.

All the while, Italy was making plans to launch a war on Ethiopia. These plans would be realized on October 3rd, 1935, when Italian forces crossed over the Mareb River, which bordered

Italian Eritrea, and pushed into Ethiopian territory. Showing the bitterness held in the collective memory of Italy, one of the first towns that the Italian troops seized was none other than Adwa—the site of their previous defeat. Here, on October 6th, they encountered the local forces of Ras Seyoum Mengesha.

It soon became clear that the Ras's militia was not prepared to withstand the Italian assault. They were especially not prepared for aerial bombardment. After just a couple of days of dealing with this onslaught, Ras Seyoum ordered his troops to abandon the city. Realizing that resistance was futile, the denizens of nearby Mekelle not only surrendered but also decided to join forces with the Italians.

The Italians already had many Ethiopians mixed in with their own troops due to recruits pulled from their colony in Eritrea, and subsequent defectors would come to increase the number of native Ethiopians in the Italian armed forces.

But although the Italians in northern Ethiopia were having an easy time, the Italian troops that had crossed from Italian Somaliland into Ethiopia were having a much more difficult go of it. Here, Ethiopian forces adapted quite well to the aerial bombardment they were subjected to by digging strategic trenches. As soon as the whine of an overhead plane was heard, troops could duck down in the trenches and avoid being hit by the blast. Their arms were sufficient to deal severe blows to the Italian troops on the ground.

However, after their valiant commander Gerazmach Afework was struck down on November 5th, both morale and the cohesion of the troops were lost. The Italians, led by notorious Italian General Rodolfo Graziani, were able to overcome the Ethiopian defenders. That same month, the League of Nations finally came around to sanctioning Italy, but it was too little, too late.

In the meantime, Haile Selassie knew he had to play his hand carefully for a variety of reasons. He intentionally told his main body of troops to pull back. He knew that by strategically pulling back, the Italians would be forced to overextend their supply lines, which would make them more vulnerable. Haile Selassie knew that the Italians had them outgunned and had better equipment and armaments. As such, he knew he had to use his resources as carefully as possible and wait for just the right moment to strike.

The Italians met little resistance, so they must have considered the invasion a walk in the park. They consolidated their gains, which included Adwa, Adigrat, Enticho, and even Tewodros's former stronghold of Magdala. The major Ethiopian counteroffensive finally came in January 1936. The Ethiopian army was divided into three main battle groups. They confronted the Italian armed forces in what would become known as the Battle of Tembein.

The Ethiopian troops fought hard, smashing into Italian possessions on all sides. At first, it seemed as if the Italians would have to retreat, but they persevered long enough to receive relief from Italian aircraft. The Italian planes altered the course of the battle by dropping poison gas on the Ethiopian troops. Soon, mustard gas was wreaking havoc in the Ethiopian ranks, with no way for them to properly defend against it. Even back then, such tactics had been banned and deemed a violation of the international rules of warfare. As such, these actions were clearly war crimes.

After the main Ethiopian army was repulsed at the Battle of Tembein, the Italians would retain the initiative for the rest of the war, scoring a string of victories. The Battle of Amba Aradam, the Second Battle of Tembein, and the Battle of the Shire would all see the Italians emerge victorious. The situation was desperate, and the battered Ethiopian army was on its last legs when, on March 31st, 1936, Hailie Selassie made the fateful decision to lead the last remnants of his troops in what would become the Battle of Maychew.

The Ethiopians fought ferociously against the Italians and managed to stall the Italian invasion, but it was a last-gasp effort. By April 3rd, the overwhelming bulk of the Italian forces concentrated on this one beleaguered group and forced the remnants of Haile Selassie's army to pull back. Haile Selassie barely escaped with his life.

Nevertheless, he returned to Addis Ababa on April 30th and met with his council to determine what could be done. It was then that it was decided that although Ethiopia was likely to lose this stage of the war against the Italians, Haile Selassie should escape. They knew that even if the Italians occupied Ethiopia, as long as Haile Selassie lived, he would hold the flame of the true Ethiopian government. And Selassie would keep the people's hope alive that Ethiopian independence could somehow be rekindled.

On May 3rd, Emperor Haile Selassie and his immediate family arrived by train in Djibouti, and the following day, he was on board a British naval craft. At this point, Addis Ababa had already fallen to the Italians. Italian General Pietro Badoglio officially proclaimed Ethiopia to be part of what he called "Italian East Africa." Haile Selassie was the only one left to carry on the fight, and if he could not do so on the battlefield, he would do so in the halls of foreign powers.

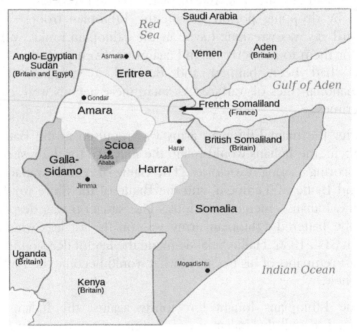

A map of Italian East Africa.

Selassie ended up disembarking in Geneva, Switzerland, the seat of the League of Nations. Once there, he spoke in front of a crowd of delegates, informing them directly of the blatant aggression and downright atrocities that the Italians had been committing in Ethiopia. Despite some crude remarks from the Italians who were present, Haile Selassie delivered a clear, detailed, eloquent speech, demanding the League of Nations live up to its charter and prevent the rogue aggression being meted out by the Italian armed forces.

The speech was a thought-provoking moment for the world. And once World War Two broke out, the world would see the Italians running amok in Africa and the Mediterranean, the Japanese devastating East Asia, and the Germans rampaging through Europe. Haile Selassie's words would then come to take on even more ominous meaning. After leaving Geneva, Switzerland, Haile Selassie sought refuge in England, taking up residence in the town of Bath. He would remain there for the next few years as his countrymen fought a guerrilla war against the occupying Italian forces and continued to wait for their day of deliverance.

World War Two would commence with the German invasion of Poland in 1939. This was followed by Germany's conquest of France in 1940. Italy's allegiance to Germany finally brought the world's attention to what Italy had been doing in Ethiopia.

British troops in nearby Sudan soon mobilized to take on the Italians in neighboring Ethiopia. In January 1941, a joint Ethiopian/British army poured out of Sudan and charged into the Italian positions. The Italians, who had a major advantage over the Ethiopians due to disparities in equipment, were no match for the British, who had arguably even better armaments than the Italians.

The Italians were decimated, and the Ethiopian/British force, with none other than Haile Selassie among the ranks, soon cut through the Italian army, pushing all the way into Addis Ababa. The Italians in Ethiopia had been defeated. But it would take some time to completely reassert Selassie's control over the nation. He was restored to power with the caveat that British troops would remain in place to safeguard the fragile rebuilding process.

The British also insisted they had the right to declare a state of emergency at any time if they felt it was necessary. Haile Selassie was back in power, but with the British around, his absolute authority had not yet been restored. There were those, no doubt, who must have feared that Ethiopia had just exchanged one colonizer for another. But the British did not have any interest in colonizing Ethiopia, and in 1944, when the Allies had World War Two almost won, Britain signed an agreement with Selassie to return his state to its pre-war conditions.

However, the British frustrated Selassie by keeping some of their troops in the easternmost region of Ethiopia, known as Ogaden. Ten years later, in 1954, Selassie would finally settle this matter with help from the United States. The US was concerned about Russian influence in Egypt and wished to use Ethiopia as a counterweight in the region. This led to the signing of an Ethiopian-US treaty in 1953. The United States would become the number one financer for the Ethiopian armed forces. The Americans also aided in the establishment of civil aviation in Ethiopia, resulting in the creation of Ethiopian Airlines.

The year 1955 was a banner year for Selassie since it was his Silver Jubilee (his twenty-fifth year of ruling Ethiopia). That year, he submitted a revised constitution that set the stage for the kind of governmental structure Selassie felt would be most viable for a modernized Ethiopia. It was along the lines of a constitutional monarchy.

Selassie wished a more centralized government would take root in Addis Ababa and then spiral out to all of the various regions. He also wished to implement greater equality among the citizens, with education, jobs, and access to the ballot box available to all Ethiopians. The ballot box, of course, applied to all positions below the monarchy since no one would be voting for who would be emperor.

Selassie's long reign would last for nearly twenty more years. It only came to an end when communist-influenced agitators known as the Derg and a certain low-ranking colonel named Mengistu toppled the Ethiopian government, toppling the long-lived and last

Ethiopian Emperor Haile Selassie from power.

Haile Selassie, one of Ethiopia's most well-known leaders.

https://en.wikipedia.org/wiki/File:Addis_Ababa-8c00855u.jpg

Chapter 9 – Enter Mengistu: Ethiopia Becomes Communist

"Henceforth we will tackle our enemies that come face to face with us and we will not be stabbed in from behind by internal foes. To this end, we will arm the allies and comrades of the broad masses without giving respite to reactionaries, and avenge the blood of our comrades double—and triple--fold."

-Mengistu Haile Mariam

It is with some irony to note that the movement to overthrow Haile Selassie had its roots in student movements. It was ironic because Haile Selassie was a champion of education. Selassie wanted to reform and modernize his country, and he naturally considered a robust education system as a means to create a class of highly skilled and sophisticated Ethiopians.

However, the hallowed halls of Ethiopia's universities would become the repository for radical discourse, such as a Marxist revolution. And it would be in the halls of academia that communism was vigorously discussed. These discussions spilled out of the classroom as activists began to openly question and even challenge government policies.

According to Ethiopian scholar Bahru Zewde, these ideas managed to reach a wider audience in Ethiopia by the mid-1960s with the establishment of the EUS (Ethiopian University Service), a special program that had college students spending time in the more rural and remote regions of Ethiopia, where they served as teachers and conducted various workshops. Interestingly enough, after Ethiopia's communist revolution, Mengistu's regime sponsored a very similar program. However, the Ethiopian communists did so with the express intent of spreading communist ideology, whereas Emperor Haile Selassie contributed to this effort entirely by accident.

All of these happenings are stunningly similar to what occurred in Russia in the 1870s under Tsar Alexander II. To be clear, Russia would not have a Marxist revolution until 1917 under Tsar Alexander II's grandson Nicholas, but the events that occurred in pre-communist Russia are strikingly similar to what happened in Ethiopia in the 1960s and 1970s.

For example, Tsar Alexander II, like Haile Selassie, was in the contradictory position of being an absolute monarch who wanted to reform and modernize Russia through educational reforms. In Russia, just like in Ethiopia, the universities became the centers of revolutionary intelligentsia. And also like in Ethiopia, the urban-based college revolutionaries managed to connect with rural peasants through teaching programs abroad. Although Russia's march to Marxism would take longer, Tsar Alexander II would end up being assassinated by the very revolutionaries his efforts of reform helped to bring about.

At any rate, as it pertained to Ethiopia, by the early 1970s, all was not well in the kingdom. War raged in Eritrea, which Ethiopia had been seeking to reassert its dominance over ever since the end of the Second World War. Ethiopia also faced an economic downturn, an episode of famine in 1972, and high gas prices due to raging conflicts in the Middle East.

These hardships fused together with radical ideology. The students took to the streets, and this time around, they were accompanied by citizens from all walks of life. Haile Selassie was caught off-guard and initially reacted to the protests by cracking down on them. He rounded up protesters and had them thrown in prison. But at this point, there were so many in the streets that the arrests had very little effect.

Things came to a head in 1974 when student protesters joined forces with taxi drivers who went on strike in Addis Ababa. The college students made matters worse by blocking traffic. Selassie realized that arresting protesters would not solve the problem, so he decided to uproot his government. On February 28th, 1974, he had his prime minister, Aklilu Habte-Wold, dismiss the whole cabinet so that they could appoint all new members.

But the revolutionaries in the street did not care about Selassie appointing new members to his cabinet. What they really wanted was an entirely new form of government. In fact, the agitators developed their own popular slogan to mock these efforts by declaring, "Changing the stove does not make the stew any better!" In their minds, Haile Selassie, who was in his eighties, was that old stove, cooking up the same old stew. These revolutionaries would not be happy until the stove—Emperor Haile Selassie—was removed from power.

A cadre of junior officers of the Ethiopian military formed a council to deal with the ongoing protests and unrest, which they called the Derg. However, instead of relieving Selassie's troubles, this shadowy group soon turned on Selassie. Many of the details of what went on behind the scenes still remain unclear, but representatives of the Derg went public on September 12th, 1974, to announce that Haile Selassie had been taken into custody.

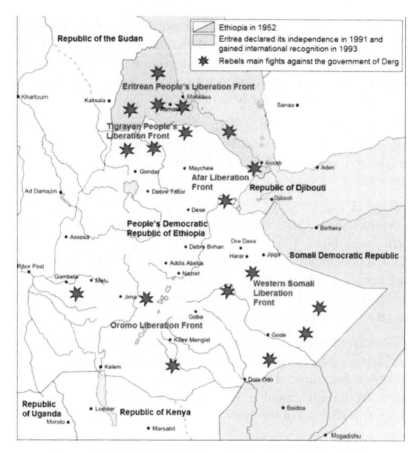

A map of the Ethiopian Civil War, which lasted from 1974 to 1991.

That December, the Derg made international headlines by revealing that Haile Selassie had considerable sums of money in a Swiss bank account. The Derg suggested the amount to be in the billions, while Swiss representatives disputed this, claiming that it was only one hundred million. It was still a large amount either way, and it was large enough to anger the general public in Ethiopia. To them, it was scandalous for the emperor to have such a hoard of wealth when the average citizen could not put gas in their car and possibly did not even have enough food to even survive.

Mengistu and his cronies demanded that the money be released to them so that they could use it for famine relief. The Swiss Bankers Association refused, stating, "We must have assurance that the agreement to make the transfer from the emperor's account was not obtained under duress."

Nevertheless, the Derg's steady drive toward communism continued. In January of 1975, it was announced that land would be divvied up and that all financial institutions would be nationalized.

The United States, for one, anxiously watched these developments, fearing that Ethiopia was about to slide into the communist bloc. These fears were heightened in March 1975 when representatives of the Derg proclaimed that the monarchy had been abolished. By then, a junior colonel by the name of Mengistu Haile Mariam came to play a more prominent role in the group, becoming a deputy chairman.

Shortly thereafter, Emperor Haile Selassie died while under the Derg's custody. To this day, not much is known about Haile Selassie's last days. However, it has long been rumored that Mengistu himself strangled the emperor and killed him. Mengistu, who is still alive, as of this writing, has denied doing this.

At any rate, Colonel Mengistu began to rise up the ranks of the revolutionary council, and by the spring of 1977, he was firmly in control. That year, the fateful Red Terror began. Ethiopians remember the inauguration of communist rule as starting at this point since it was during this time that lands were aggressively seized, and citizens were routinely oppressed and brutalized. During this reign of terror, it is estimated that at least 500,000 Ethiopians were killed, and countless more were locked up in prisons all throughout the country.

Yes, as is so often the case with radical ideologues, these revolutionaries who roundly condemned Emperor Haile Selassie as being oppressive quickly began inflicting their own version of oppression, the likes of which the average Ethiopian had never before seen. They had promised a utopia in Ethiopia but brought only terror to the people.

Chapter 10 – The Fall of Communism and the Rise of Modern Ethiopia

"Many Ethiopians see yesterday. I see tomorrow."

-Abiy Ahmed

Just as soon as the communist regime in Ethiopia began, there were those who resisted it and wished to see its demise. Some of the resistance came from those who were against Marxist ideology, but surprisingly enough, the Derg was vigorously resisted by other Marxist groups, most notably the Tigray People's Liberation Front (TPLF), which espoused Marxist beliefs. The party was founded in 1977, and from the outset, it was in opposition to the Mengistu-controlled Derg.

The TPLF would be an even more troubling thorn in Mengistu's side since it would join forces with another opposition group based out of Eritrea, the EPLF or Eritrean People's Liberation Front. If the name "people's liberation front," which is a hallmark of grassroots Marxist fronts all over the world, does not give it away, a quick look at the original platforms of both of these groups clearly demonstrates that they were Marxist through and through.

Yet, all the same, they opposed the communist regime that took root in Addis Ababa. The EPLF, in particular, was essentially a nationalistic group that sought to break away from Ethiopia. Ever since Eritrea had been returned to Ethiopia after World War Two, the Eritreans had incessantly attempted to break away. Emperor Haile Selassie was constantly putting down insurgences, and so would Mengistu. All communist leanings aside, the EPLF was yet another variation of insurgents fighting for Eritrean independence.

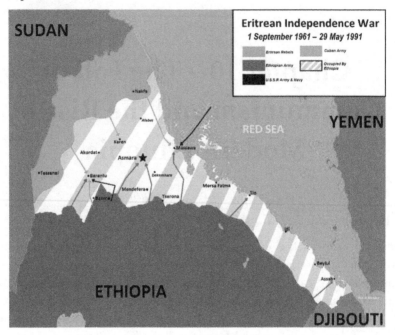

A basic overview of what territories looked like during the Eritrean War of Independence.

The TPLF of Tigray, which borders Eritrea, found a common cause with the EPLF, and they began to work closely together. The TPLF caused trouble for the Derg regime by regularly hampering travel on roads that crossed through Tigray into Eritrea. The EPLF also took the initiative by gaining de facto control of much of the eastern portion of Eritrea. This forced the Derg to take military action. These developments were viewed with great dismay by many since the Derg had promised to end the fighting in Eritrea. Yet the quagmire continued.

Despite all of the promises of a Marxist paradise, essentially nothing had changed for the better, and many aspects of life were actually much worse. Famine even returned worse than before in the early 1980s. Although Ethiopia had lost the official support and backing of the United States after becoming communist, many non-governmental organizations took notice, and charitable efforts were made.

A view of the Live Aid stage in Philadelphia, Pennsylvania.

Most notably, a huge benefit concert called Live Aid was held in 1985 in which superstar musicians and celebrities performed for huge crowds to raise money for Ethiopians suffering from the terrible famine. Sadly, it is unclear how much these efforts helped since most of the proceeds were likely pocketed by the Derg regime, which used it to finance military operations against the TPLF and EPLF in northern Ethiopia. Superstar musicians, such as Bruce Springsteen and Michael Jackson, no doubt meant well and can hardly be blamed for trying. But as much as folks were touched by all of those heartfelt renditions of "We are the world," governments around the world had good reason not to deal with the Mengistu regime. They knew that any funds that were delivered would no doubt end up in Mengistu Haile Mariam's pockets.

Along with having to fight off insurgents in northern Ethiopia, the Mengistu regime had to face off against Somalian troops in Ethiopia's eastern Ogaden region. Conflict first broke out between the two countries in 1977, and its onset entirely perplexed Ethiopia's and Somalia's Soviet backers.

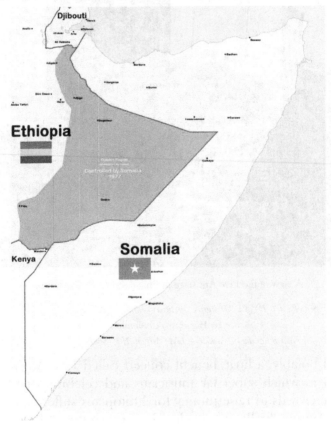

Ethiopian territory occupied by Somalia, 1977.

At this time, both Ethiopia and Somalia were in the communist camp and backed by the Soviet Union. The Soviets were shocked that two communist nations would fight each other, but it was no more shocking than the Ethiopian communist regime of Addis Ababa fighting communist guerrillas from the TPLF and EPLF in the north. The Ogaden War with Somalia ended with an Ethiopian victory in 1978, but the crisis in the north would continue to weigh heavily on the Derg regime.

In early 1982, Mengistu led a large military campaign into northern Ethiopia in an attempt to root out these insurgents. But by the end of the year, the EPLF had rallied and began to push back the government's troops, resulting in a large loss of life. In the end, this defeat left Mengistu's regime with over ten thousand dead soldiers and nothing to show for it. However, this would pale in comparison to those killed in the famine that first erupted in the fall of 1983.

The famine was largely brought about by the failed policy of farming collectives introduced by the communist regime. Mengistu and his cronies sought to create communal farms to boost agricultural production in Ethiopia. But drought coupled with severe mismanagement ultimately led to a disastrous famine that would lead to mass starvation. It is almost hard to believe, but according to Ethiopian scholar Harold Marcus, by 1984, around ten thousand Ethiopians were dying in the severely affected Wollo Province on a weekly basis.

Initially, Mengistu's government's strategy in confronting the crisis was to pretend it did not exist. As bad as things were in the more remote provinces, the crisis began to rock Addis Ababa by the summer of 1984 when the lack of production from the rural regions translated into a lack of food on the shelves of grocery stores in the capital. And what little food there was left began to see their prices skyrocket as inflation took hold. Soon, simply buying a loaf of bread was beyond the means of the average Ethiopian.

Nevertheless, the Mengistu regime, rather than addressing the crisis, spent more time planning the celebration of the Derg's tenth anniversary of coming to power. After the celebrations came to a close, Mengistu, who was already running the regime anyway, was officially elected as general secretary, commander in chief of the armed forces, and chairman of the council of ministers. These were just a bunch of meaningless titles for a man who had already been the de facto dictator of Ethiopia anyway.

After Mengistu's "promotion," he began to let the wider world in on the famine problem. The BBC was allowed access to the stricken areas, and soon the whole world was aware of the terrible famine in Ethiopia, with Ethiopian civilians starving to death on a daily basis. International aid suddenly flowed in, supplying surplus grain to feed the starving Ethiopians.

These efforts did help Ethiopia through the worst of the crisis. But as the debacle of Live Aid would demonstrate, international aid organizations were wise to unload bags of grain rather than bags of cash. Grain could be sent to starving villages, but the bags of cash meant to purchase food would disappear into the greedy hands of the regime. Along with pocketing cash, Mengistu also used the time-worn, cynical tactic of blocking food aid from reaching certain rebel strongholds, hoping to starve his opponents into submission.

Nevertheless, Ethiopia managed to survive the famine, and by 1985, the worst of it had passed. The war with the TPLF and EPLF would continue. The EPLF would make shocking gains in late 1987 when its troops managed to drive deep into what had previously been uncontested territory. There was a distinct collapse in the morale of Mengistu's troops, and by the spring of 1988, defection was a major problem.

At this point, many of Mengistu's generals thought that the war with Eritrea was lost and that some sort of compromise should be made. One of Mengistu's generals apparently voiced these concerns a bit too loudly for Mengistu's liking, as the dictator had him executed. Despite the grave concerns expressed by his commanders, Mengistu pushed his battered and weary army on.

In the next round of major fighting, in March 1988, the Ethiopian troops received a devastating blow when an entire division was almost completely annihilated by the EPLF. But far more devastating to the regime, even more than the loss of life, was the loss of military equipment. It is said that after this defeat, the EPLF was able to seize some fifty tanks and a large cache of artillery, RPGs, and all manner of firearms that had been left behind by the fleeing government troops.

This greatly emboldened the EPLF, and soon, they were coordinating a massive strike against the Ethiopian government with their TPLF partners. A major offensive in northern Ethiopia ensued, and by that April, the EPLF had essentially taken over all of northern Eritrea. Government forces attempted to rebound and cross into Eritrea from Tigray, only to have the TPLF sneak up behind them and turn them into target practice.

The government troops were routed, and the TPLF took the initiative and seized several historic towns in northern Ethiopia, such as Aksum (Axum) and Adwa.

As the TPLF made increasing gains, the government troops were forced to fall back and retreat from Tigray altogether. Soon, wounded soldiers and refugees began to flood into the capital, and the regime had to admit it was locked in a bloody stalemate with the rebel fighters. The Ethiopian public was outraged at the government's failures, and there was talk amongst high-level members of the army about ousting Mengistu from power.

However, Mengistu learned of their plotting and dismissed all of those who had spoken out against him. The sacking of top generals only exacerbated the problems the military faced, as they were replaced by inexperienced commanders, leading to incompetence on the battlefield when an effective and clear strategy was needed more than ever.

The year 1989 was a fateful one, as it saw the collapse of communism in Eastern Europe. Ethiopia's former communist backer, the Soviet Union, was quite preoccupied since it was forced to deal with the fall of the Berlin Wall and the disintegration of much of the USSR. Mengistu knew that the Russians would no longer be of service and sought to somehow change with the times. He wished to convert his Marxist regime into a hybrid mixed economy system that would end the one-party rule and embrace democracy.

On March 5th, 1990, Mengistu, who was desperately clinging to power by any means, went as far as to proclaim that there would be an "end to socialism." This trick would not work, and Mengistu soon realized his time was up. The TPLF, the EPLF, and other rebel groups joined forces to form the Ethiopian People's Revolutionary Democratic Front or EPRDF. They sent a massive army to march on the capital of Addis Ababa in May of 1991. Mengistu, for all of his stonewalling, finally understood that it was over.

Tanks that had been left behind after the capital was taken, 1991.

Mengistu ended up fleeing Ethiopia and received safe haven in Zimbabwe. The EPRDF took control of the country and installed a provisional government. Under the provisional government, Eritrea was finally granted independence in 1993. The man who would rise to the top of Ethiopian politics was TPLF leader Meles Zenawi, who was made president of the provisional government.

Meles was made the president of a so-called "transitional government," but he ended up staying on as a life-long leader until he passed away in 2012. He was elected under questionable conditions as the prime minister of Ethiopia in 1995 and would repeatedly be elected under conditions that his critics decried as being "rigged."

The most documented claims of electoral malfeasance took place in the 2005 election when thousands took to the streets protesting against what they saw as voter fraud. Leaders of opposition parties claimed that Meles Zenawi's cronies had vigorously tampered with polling stations all over Ethiopia.

According to the official results, Meles Zenawi had won in a landslide, but according to the massive number of protesters on the street, this was likely more fantasy than reality. Nevertheless, Meles Zenawi only had one response for those who dared claim there was anything afoot in the election. His response was an immediate and brutal crackdown, officially banning all demonstrations and arresting—and in some instances even killing—anyone who dared to protest.

Before it was all said and done, protesters were locked up in droves, and an astonishing 193 of them were killed by Ethiopian police. There were once again claims of election fraud in 2010, but this time, the demonstrations were much less vigorous, seemingly indicating that Meles Zenawi's previous brutal crackdowns had been effective. From here on out, it seemed that Meles Zenawi's grip on power was secure, and he would remain in charge until his abrupt demise in 2012.

Meles Zenawi most certainly had his critics, and after his death, many average Ethiopians on the street would tell you that he was a straight-up dictator hiding under the guise of a fraudulent democratic process. But nevertheless, it was under Meles that the current incarnation of the Ethiopian government—the Federal Democratic Republic of Ethiopia—was forged.

Conclusion: Ethiopia Today

After the death of long-time Ethiopian Prime Minister Meles Zenawi in 2012, a new prime minister by the name of Hailemariam Desalegn was appointed. Desalegn and his party went on to do quite well in the 2015 election, but the political opposition called election procedures into question, and massive unrest ensued. This culminated in major protests rocking much of Ethiopia in the summer of 2016.

Things were so bad that the Ethiopian government declared a state of emergency, which would last until August of 2017. The situation did not improve much when the emergency measures were lifted, and tired and weary Prime Minister Hailemariam Desalegn ended up calling it quits, tendering his resignation in February 2018. This was a first in Ethiopia since no previous Ethiopian leader (unless you count Mengistu fleeing from the country) had ever willingly and intentionally left the highest office of the land of their own accord.

After Desalegn washed his hands of Ethiopian politics, chaos once again ensued. Yet another state of martial law was declared, which would remain in place until the new prime minister—Abiy Ahmed—was elected and took office. Abiy Ahmed's tenure has been controversial, to say the least. He was hailed early on as a great communicator and peacemaker. In fact, he was awarded the Nobel Peace Prize in 2019.

But since then, many have called his actions into question. Admittedly, Prime Minister Abiy Ahmed was dealt a very weak hand upon gaining office and had inherited many troubling circumstances. Ethiopia's regional conflicts were on the rise, and there was massive unrest in the traditionally ethnic Oromo regions of the south and the ethnic Tigrayan regions of the north. The latter would end up causing Abiy Ahmed the most significant crisis of his administration, as it led to an all-out civil war with Tigray Province.

The problem began during the 2020 pandemic when Abiy Ahmed delayed national elections. Such a move would be viewed with suspicion in many countries. Even in the United States, when the idea of delaying the election was briefly floated, it received massive and immediate pushback and quickly became an impossibility.

Yet, Ethiopian Prime Minister Abiy Ahmed cited concerns over the pandemic and went ahead and called for a delay in national voting. In blatant defiance of Abiy's order, the leaders of Tigray went ahead and voted anyway, hosting regional elections on September 9th, 2020.

The situation then simmered until November 4th, when TPLF forces launched a major offensive against Ethiopian troops stationed in Tigray. This event triggered the Ethiopian Civil War, which, as of 2022, still rages. The fighting has wavered back and forth since its outbreak, and both sides have claimed war crimes against the other. Until this bloody conflict comes to a close, the future of Ethiopia remains to be determined.

Here's another book by
Captivating History that you might like

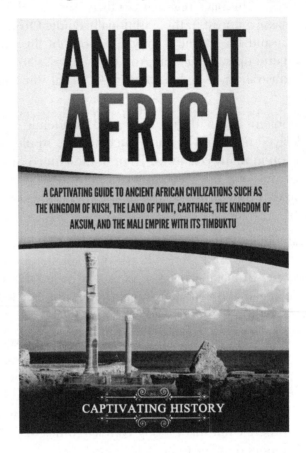

Free Bonus from Captivating History (Available for a Limited time)

Hi History Lovers!

Now you have a chance to join our exclusive history list so you can get your first history ebook for free as well as discounts and a potential to get more history books for free! Simply visit the link below to join.

Captivatinghistory.com/ebook

Also, make sure to follow us on Facebook, Twitter and Youtube by searching for Captivating History.

Appendix A: Further Reading and Reference

Ethiopia: Land of the Conquering Lion of Judah. Edmonds, I. G. 1975.

Ethiopia: The Unknown Land. Munro-Hay, S. C. 2002.

The Abyssinians. Buxton, David. 1970.

A History of Modern Ethiopia: 1855-1991. Zewde, Bahru. 2001.

A History of Ethiopia. Marcus, Harold, G. 1994.